Freya Stark (1893–1993), '
of travel', was the doyenne of
East travel writers and one of
courageous and adventurous women
travellers   the
travelled extensively throughout Syria,
Palestine, Lebanon, Iran, Iraq and
Southern Arabia, where she became
the first western woman to travel
through the Hadhramaut. Usually
alone, she ventured to places few
Europeans had visited. Her travels
earned her the title of Dame and huge
public acclaim. Her many, now classic,

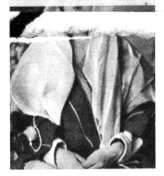

books include *Traveller's Prelude, Ionia, The Southern Gates of
Arabia, Alexander's Path, Dust in the Lion's Paw, East is West* and
Valleys of the Assassins.

'It's hard to think of a writer in the travel game who most closely demonstrates the merits of Flaubert's three rules for good writing: clarity, clarity and finally clarity. Re-reading her now, her restrained powers of description shine as brightly as they ever did, and they will continue to shine until the next Ice Age . . . Her books are more relevant than ever. Besides sheer enjoyment, one should read her for a fresh perspective on the intractable issues dogging Christian-Muslim relations. She was able to see both sides and what she found was similarity, not difference. The greatest woman traveller of the 20th century? I think so.'   Sara Wheeler, *The Times*

'It was rare to leave her company without feeling that the world was somehow larger and more promising. Her life was something of a work of art. . . . The books in which she recorded her journeys were seductively individual. . . . Nomad and social lioness, public servant and private essayist, emotional victim and mythmaker.'
                                Colin Thubron, *New York Times*

'Few writers have the capacity to do with words what Fabergé could do with gems – to fashion them, without violating their quality. It is this extraordinary talent which sets Freya Stark apart from her fellow craftsman in the construction of books on travel.'
                                The *Daily Telegraph*

'Freya Stark remains unexcelled as an interpreter of brief encounters in wild regions against the backdrop of history.'   The *Observer*

'One of the finest travel writers of our century.'   *The New Yorker*

'A Middle East traveler, an explorer and, above all, a writer, Freya Stark has, with an incomparably clear eye, looked toward the horizon of the past without ever losing sight of the present. Her books are route plans of a perceptive intelligence, traversing time and space with ease.'   *Saudi Aramco World*

Tauris Parke Paperbacks is an imprint of I.B.Tauris. It is dedicated to publishing books in accessible paperback editions for the serious general reader within a wide range of categories, including biography, history, travel and the ancient world. The list includes select, critically acclaimed works of top quality writing by distinguished authors that continue to challenge, to inform and to inspire. These are books that possess those subtle but intrinsic elements that mark them out as something exceptional.

The Colophon of Tauris Parke Paperbacks is a representation of the ancient Egyptian ibis, sacred to the god Thoth, who was himself often depicted in the form of this most elegant of birds. Thoth was credited in antiquity as the scribe of the ancient Egyptian gods and as the inventor of writing and was associated with many aspects of wisdom and learning.

THE ZODIAC ARCH

Freya Stark

TPP

TAURIS PARKE
PAPERBACKS

New paperback edition published in 2014 by Tauris Parke Paperbacks
An imprint of I.B.Tauris and Co Ltd
6 Salem Road, London W2 4BU
175 Fifth Avenue, New York NY 10010
www.ibtauris.com

Distributed in the United States and Canada Exclusively by Palgrave Macmillan
175 Fifth Avenue, New York NY 10010

First published in 1968 by John Murray (Publishers) Limited

ISBN: 978 1 78076 688 1

A full CIP record for this book is available from the British Library
A full CIP record is available from the Library of Congress

Library of Congress Catalog Card Number: available

Printed and bound in England by CPI Group (UK) Ltd, Croydon, CR0 4YY

MIX
Paper from
responsible sources
FSC
www.fsc.org   FSC® C013604

This book is dedicated to
Lucy and Alan Moorehead
with deep affection

Contents

Preface

No one will quarrel with a patchwork quilt if the materials it is made of are adequate, and I hope the same indulgence may be given to this book. Its essays have mostly been published, the only unpublished portion being that of three short stories and some chapters at the end. They are as disconnected as objects piled in a bazaar, and have the same sort of idleness – for what can be more chancy than the thoughts of human beings, leaping from one thing to another? A fakir will keep them steady by repeating the same words, but that would be a poor performance for an essayist, and dull for the reader; and our aim, I take it, is the one we enjoy in life in general – an interest enlivened by curiosity and held to its bearings by some awareness of what lies beyond the human horizon out of sight.

This is what I should like my essays to achieve. They do not always succeed, and many fall to browsing by the way. Looking over their unequal ranks, I came to the conclusion that the only link between them was that of 'Time'. It is interesting, if one reads an author at all, to watch his methods developing, and this volume – which opens in Baghdad in 1932 with a certain inexpert optimism and does indeed go back to 1917 in the short stories – has therefore a span of half a century. To find oneself coherent after such a long diet of variety is very surprising.

During these fifty years two wars have involved everyone we knew and all we cared for, and we have seen our Empire, the greatest since Rome, rise to its pinnacle and fall away. Whatever future hopes we may cherish, there is bound to be, for us who saw this happen, a time of sorrow before a fresh day rises to whatever new skyline it may find. The sorrow exists, but seems to have left only the faintest echo in these casual papers, and their lesson, if they have one, is cheerful: whatever masonry was crumbling, the butterflies still fluttered under Titus' arch; a splash of shadow hit them now and then, but the greater shadows are out of sight, not unnoticed but unattended. Because of their existence, which should not be forgotten, and so as to link these random thoughts in something of a chain, I have inserted a few paragraphs of explanation, here and there between one digression and the next.

The series begins in a period of light-hearted trifling, in 1932 with no cloud on the horizon, when I made my living – just – by writing for kind Mr Cameron on the *Baghdad Times*.

S. Zenone degli Ezzelini,
Autumn 1967

The Foreign Office 'H'

When I came to my office the other day, with that anticipation of instruction and delight which the prolonged study of Reuter telegrams may be presumed to foster, I saw among the papers on my desk a typewritten sheet signed with a rubber stamp, 'British Embassy, Bagdad' – just Bagdad, without an H, as it might be Ollywood or Littleampton.

I was shocked.

Can it be possible, I thought, that this august document has lain so long among the Reuter telegrams that it has acquired their peculiar notions of the English language?

Or is it a Diplomatic Incident? Without its H, Bagdad means nothing at all; but with it, it is derived by Arab historians from the Persian as signifying a 'garden of Justice'. It is nice for a place to be called a garden of Justice, whether it is one or not. The Foreign Office might of course not think of us as such: and it might, of course, always want to say exactly what it thinks: and so it might be saying it in a diplomatic way through a philological insinuation.

Or perhaps it is just that the Foreign Office does not know how to spell?

Spelling, we admit, is one of those accomplishments that diplomacy need not trouble about: and geography is often proved to be beneath the notice of public men. With any other letter of the alphabet it would not matter. But H has a peculiar position all its own. It has acquired the dignity and mystery of a symbol. Years of expensive ancestors or training are necessary to its proper management.

'The little H, and how much it is.' Put it were it is not not whanted and nobody whill believe that you have been educated at Arrow or Heton.

To see our Foreign Office forgetting itself in a body as it were, dropping its h's and giving us a cockney Bagdad on its own rubber stamp, is a humiliating experience for British patriots in Iraq. 'Gh' has long been recognized by all the best people as the only possible transliteration for that Arabic sound which otherwise can only be expressed by the clearing of one's throat before a cough.

The Foreign Office cannot be expected to discover such minor details by itself, especially now that it is chronically busy with these Conferences that are always beginning so well. But there must be some little office boy in Downing Street who could rush into the library between one thing and another and turn over the leaves of an etymological dictionary: and at the worst, could run round and ask the Royal Geographical Society, who have a committee thinking out transliterations all their lives, and apparently enjoying it. Delighted to spell the most difficult names, and capable of reading even a German transliterator without fainting, they would listen with patience and urbanity to whatever enormity the Foreign Office might put before them.

1932

The love for Persia, which pulls at my heart every year in spring, first came in one romantic wave as I drove to the highlands of Karind and crossed the ranges, and settled for a few months' study in Hamadan. This ancient Ecbatana was in those days a small, poor and sprawling town, with a torrent steeply tumbling by the High Street, and never a tourist in sight; and I stayed while the cold April storms, I can just remember, blossomed into a fretwork of orchards with the sun shining through them, transparent as alabaster and brittle as glass.

Persian Legends

M irza Husein, my Persian teacher, his insignificant body submerged in flowing draperies, his small intelligent eyes a-twinkle while he uttered the pious platitudes in which his soul delighted, would come every evening during my stay in Hamadan, and while the dusk made the white falling petals seem luminous in the garden, and the clouds gathered and hurled themselves in storms over the Asadabad pass and the ridges of Elvand, would sit with a leg hitched under him to lessen the discomfort of European chairs, and freeing one hand from its many long sleeves to take fresh cigarettes at frequent intervals, would tell me legends of the Shi'as.

As his business in life was that of a public letter-writer, he sat all day in a small dark recess in the outer wall of the court of the great mosque in Hamadan, and there he drew up legal documents of every kind and contracts of marriage or divorce for such clients as came along.

'When they come to marry I encourage them,' said he. 'And when they divorce I give them good advice. But it is not much use,' he added.

Sometimes, divorces being frequent in Hamadan, he would say that he was tired of giving good advice – in a bad world; and the word *bad,* the same in Persian and English, had a peculiar force in the Mirza's mouth, as if he had discovered in it a new and painful meaning of his own.

Usually he was a little late, and would step briskly through the garden with his book of canon law wrapped in a napkin and his cloak billowing out beneath the white neatness of his turban like the russet sails of fishing boats filled by a sunset breeze when they make for their

Adriatic harbours. So would he sail up, his hennaed beard the same sunset colour; his whole bearing showing by its gravity the estimation in which he held himself. It was amusing to watch him with the Chief of Police, who fed at our inn and had no use for insects such as scribes, and would stand in the garden path, with black top-boots apart to support the massive weight of khaki up above, with the lion of Persia on his brown *kolback* pushed back – for it began to be warm – so that it stood passant over an expanse of baldness; and in this position he would look down on the little Mirza from all the altitude of Ignorance in power, while the Man of Letters, pouring his longest adjectives in an effusive stream and curling himself half over in his anxiety to please, yet managed to give the impression that Mirza Husein, who knew the Qur'an and the Traditions, was infinitely the superior of the two.

His turban was spotless. He had a special permit to wear it from the Governor of Hamadan. It was the symbol of the things now passing, a flag planted above the 'badness' of the world. On the very first evening of our acquaintance, and immediately after the important question of fees had been adjusted, he asked me whether I would prefer my teacher to come in a turban or in the new Pahlevi hat, and my choice was the beginning of our friendship.

On one particular evening I was late, having been detained by a surprising sight in Hamadan high street, which was decorated for the Shah's anniversary. The carpets were hung out, the gramophones were going full blast, and little tight bouquets, which the Persians love, ornamented everything, from the horses' tails to the sour milk in its peacock blue bowls on the stalls. But the pictures arrested me. Everyone had hung out whatever he had on either side of his front door, and the street from one end to the other was bright with mid-Victorian oleographs. I walked along fascinated, recognizing one after the other the friends of my childhood: the 'Seven Ages of Man', and the plump girl in a bustle who holds a dove to her breast; 'Othello', and 'The Babes in the Wood', and 'The Happy Family' with Papa in a check hunting suit and whiskers, and a German schloss in the background; crowned heads of all descriptions, since abdicated or dead; and children without number in pink frocks stiff as their bouquets; and the 'Little Princes in the Tower'; and 'Life among the Laplanders'. I could hardly tear myself away and, finally hurrying back past Avicenna's tomb, I found the Mirza already seated in the garden, with his hands folded inside his sleeves, in meditation by the long tank where the petals of apricot blossom float on their own reflections in the water.

'Man is a creature of hurry', said he when I had apologized. 'I will tell you what the angel said, for it deals with our father Adam.'

He pulled out his glasses and put them on in a manner which showed that there are some exceptions to the general haste of mankind, and proceeded:

'The writing has come down that Adam was moulded out of mud by the angels, and then he lay for two hundred years, before God called the spirit to enter into him. And the spirit entered in at his head. And when it reached his eyes, they saw. And when it reached his nose, it smelt. And when it reached his ears and his mouth, they heard and tasted. But when it reached his heart, and it began to feel, it could not understand that the rest of him was not yet alive, and he tried to sit up and fell back. And the angels said "Man is a creature of hurry".'

The Mirza was very poor. During the heavy April showers the roof of his small rabbit-hutch of a house fell in.

The roofs in Hamadan are mud, plastered and rolled and, in spring-time, covered deep in feathery white flowers that dance in the wind. When they collapse, the house is, as it were, smothered in its own garden plot, and I wondered what happened to the Mirza's never-mentioned wife who was supposed to live inside (washing his turbans, I imagined).

He himself lost nearly a week, first collecting two beams for a new roof, then finding men with donkeys who had a little time to spare for the conveying of mud and straw and faggots; arid finally, when all was provided, entering into negotiations with a mason. I helped a little in this crisis, and Mirza Husein took my small offering with the same admirable dignity with which he had accepted former defeats; his manner relegated these matters to the un-important limbo of transitory things.

'The Presence, the Amir,' he said, reaching his favourite subject and forgetting the day's vexations, the meagre supper of lettuce and sour milk eaten beneath a dripping roof, and all the difficulties of living in this ephemeral world, 'Our lord Ali the Amir was beset and surrounded by enemies when he dwelt in Kufa. One day three thousand men conspired to kill him when he bent to put his forehead to the ground in prayer, and each took his sword beneath his cloak and waited till he bent down in praise of God, the Exalted: then they drew their swords and lo! they held in their hands only the hilts; the blades were not there, and they went home ashamed. But one of his friends asked Ali what had become of the swords, and he said: "Go early tomorrow morning and meet a caravan outside the city gate: tell its master to hand it over and bring it to the *maidan*." And the man did so, and met the caravan, and the master riding at its head was an angel in disguise, and handed him the leading rope and vanished. And Ali's friend brought it to the *maidan* where Ali himself and all the men of Kufa were gathered. And they opened the bales on the ground and behold – the blades of three thousand swords. They put them up for sale, and the three thousand conspirators came to buy each his own sword-blade, and the Presence, the Amir, gave all that money to the poor. The generous man is honoured. And as for those who give,' said the Mirza, 'they do good to their own hearts. But as for misers and gossipers and those who ill-treat their parents, there is a writing above the gates of Paradise to say that they shall be excluded.'

The Mirza and I first discovered each other over the story of Abraham. I had come across it in travellers' books, and had then heard it in the Shammar tents; and when I made some casual reference to one of the traditions, the Mirza looked up in surprise and asked if I was interested in these 'matters of learning'.

'I know about Abraham's childhood,' said I, 'when he was hidden in the cave and fed himself by sucking milk and honey from his own finger-tips, and how he came to destroy the images of his father the maker of idols, and to believe in the one God; but of his later life I know only that which is written in our own traditions.'

'And that is very inadequate,' said the Mirza, with a note of contempt which he was usually careful to hide. 'Ours is the complete story, and it is mentioned in the Qur'an, where as you know you can find the root of everything that exists. That is why we honour it, and when we move into a new house we take over the Qur'an before any other furniture, together with a jug of water the giver of life, and a mirror, which is like an eye in the house, and some bit of greenery. But as for Abraham, you know that after marrying Sarah he travelled with her into the lands of Damascus. She was so beautiful that he was afraid, and made her travel in a big box with holes in it to see and breathe through, and when anyone approached he would lower a curtain so that she might be hidden. They reached the borders of a kingdom which lay upon their road and the Shah rode up to collect his dues in taxes before he would let them take their flocks through his land, and as the flocks were going by, he saw the box and asked to know what was inside it. "I will give half my goods," said Abraham, "if thou wilt not look." But the Shah insisted, and opened the box, and when he saw Sarah and her loveliness he asked "Who is this?" And Abraham said: "My sister." (She was his sister in religion, commented Mirza Husein, the casuist.) Then the Shah stretched forth his hand to pull her out, and Abraham was angry and turned his head away not to see, and the Shah's arm withered up to the elbow and beyond. The Shah perceived that Abraham must be a man of importance, and he asked him to restore his arm, and Abraham prayed and said: "Lord, if he is sincere, let his arm be made whole". And the Shah meant what he said, and the arm was healed.'

The Muslims are naturally not so much interested in Isaac, and the Mirza's story about him was so like our version that it is not worth repeating except for one genuine and charming bedouin touch. When the angels came as guests ('They can take on any form,' said the Mirza, 'except that of a pig or a dog,') there was nothing in the tents to offer them except one little calf which Sarah, being sorrowful and childless, had kept as a pet of her own. And so they killed the calf and gave it to their guests, because it was the best thing they had.

'The Imams,' said the Mirza, reverting to the histories of the Shi'as, 'are not really in the places of their burial, for they rise and leave them on the third day, and their tombs are only here for remembrance. The Hidden Imam is among us even now, walking about on the world. I myself have seen him twice.'

'How was that?' said I.

'The first time was at Jaffa, for you know that I embarked there for the Hajj, and as I was walking alone near the edge of the sea, suddenly there was a man where no man had been, and I felt a hotness all over me, and I knew it was the Imam. He said: "Keep thy heart firm, O Husein, for the world is bad, but thou art among the good".'

'Was that all he said?' I asked, for the Mirza was so deeply lost in the flattering recollection that the conversation seemed to be coming to an end.

'That was all,' said the Mirza, rather hurt. 'I looked again, and there was no one.'

'But what did he look like?' said I.

'He was a young man, beautiful, white like a Frank.'

'And how was he dressed?'

'His clothes?' said the Mirza, somewhat at a loss and in his heart consigning Western curiosity to the devil. 'His clothes were European but' – for I suppose I looked disappointed – 'he had long loose sleeves.' And he wore a fez,' he added, anxious to make the best of it.

After this peculiar description, which we both felt was not one of the Mirza's best efforts, we tacitly dropped the appearance of the Hidden Imam, and I asked after the second manifestation.

'That was in Mecca,' said the Mirza, restored to equanimity. 'I felt a hand touch me on the shoulder and a hotness all over me, and I knew it was the Imam. And I looked, turning my head, so, and there was a tall young man close behind me, but he said nothing, and when I looked he was not there.

'But when he appears publicly to all men it will be as a shepherd in the land of Mecca, and Gabriel will come down to him with seventy thousand angels; and three hundred and thirteen servants will descend riding on clouds above the aeroplanes. And Umar and Abu Bakr – the Imam will take their bodies out of their graves in Medina, and hang them on a dry tree: for they were idolaters.'

The Mirza bent forward to emphasize this astonishing statement, his puny little body strung taut with hatred.

'Under their cloaks they used to conceal small images of false gods, and Uthman and Khalid ibn al-Walid also, and when the Presence, the

Amir [Ali] mentioned it to the Presence, the Messenger [Muhammad], he answered: "I know it. But I will give them time." But the time of the Imam's appearance no one knows – and if they say they know, they lie,' said the Mirza with all the apparent ferocity of truth.

'And now, if your Presence will command me to take my leave, the call for prayer has sounded.'

1931

In 1936 there was already a darkening sky over Europe, an uneasiness of which many symptoms are repeating themselves, to our disquiet today. Living as I did abroad, in Fascist Italy, in what had seemed to me even from the early twenties an intolerable constriction, I can remember being more aware of the totalitarian threat than most of my friends in England at that time. The cheerful optimism of the following essay was founded on ignorance – but it was not ill-founded; it shows no inkling of the fatal flaw, so carefully kept from us by Mr Baldwin, that our armament was nil: but, apart from this unsuspected factor, it recognized what is now frequently forgotten and was then evident – the fact that a theory of empire was then being transformed in our hands into something suitable to a new age, vital and successful.

So strong was the impulse, that its essence survives both the war and the empire which brought it into being – as if a halo were to survive its head. In 1936 it was an unobtrusive revolution which those very civil servants were carrying through who, too often, have had to bear the blame for what they themselves were dedicated to destroy. Chaos came and ruined their labours: but in 1936 they were hopeful, disinterested and successful, on that smooth and shining race of water that comes before the cataract.

Ideas and the Mandate

Anyone who has motored between many frontiers on the Continent, must have pondered, during the waits which this entails, on the thing that frontiers are, so clumsy and tangible an expression of differences so subtle and intangible, so slightly graduated that at no one point, apart from uniforms and outward paraphernalia, can one say: 'This is at an end and this other begins'.

But when we reach Dover or Croydon the old insularity still holds; the physical barrier is a mental barrier also; and at the present moment we greet it with a certain complacency and its atmosphere of solidity is restful after the kaleidoscope abroad.

Our smugness must be exasperating to foreigners, but we have, in fact, something to be complacent about just now. Not, surely, a sheer monopoly of virtue: nor Democracy – a platform word: but an idiosyncrasy that makes us, so to speak, unique, though I hesitate to attribute to it the whole of our prosperity, sanity and general comfort. We are almost the only nation (or set of nations, for the Dominions must be included) who do not take their intelligentsia seriously.

*   *   *   *   *

What do we see when we look at the melancholy picture of Europe? Theorists who unfortunately have been able to put their theories into practice. Eliminate them, and the populations of Russia, Germany, Italy, Spain or Danzig are peace-loving, humdrum people, content with the ordinary affairs of life and a little spice of gossip or a murder now and then; it is not of them that our public man was thinking when he said on some platform or other that 'foreigners are always troublesome, but just now they are being more troublesome than usual'. It is the man with ideas who is reducing life on the Continent to a heap of ashes. The Fascist, Bolshevik and Nazi régimes tacitly admit it by relying for support and chiefly concentrating on the very young, on those untried spirits 'who do their work and know it not', who still believe in millenniums – communist, totalitarian or mere Utopian, as the case may be – who, in fact, have not yet ceased to expect the absolute.

We have not made the continental mistake. We have an intelligentsia, and allow, indeed encourage, it to talk and write. But it gets no more attention than does the song of the thrush or the croaking of frogs – less than the former, in fact, since most people like listening to thrushes. What I mean to say is that no Englishman in his senses, when he has serious business on hand, will stop to listen to what the highbrows are saying about it; the very word 'intelligentsia' – what subtle look of inferiority, of alien and contagious morbidity does it not wear in a page of honest Saxon prose?

I think this is what makes us incomprehensible abroad. Our embittered intellectuals, seeing that no one attends to them, cry ever more loudly; they say things that would send a Balkan republic sky-high or prevent a dictator from enjoying his breakfast . . . and nothing happens. The disillusioned Continental, sitting at his café and reading whatever extracts from the British Press happen to be favoured by his Government, is like a man who sees a fuse lighted over and over again and is never gratified by an explosion. The very knowledge of their innocuousness probably induces in our highbrows less self-restraint than they might otherwise practise: if he expected to be listened to, even G.B.S. might hesitate to commit his name to uninvestigated facts: as it is, he is allowed to be read in Italy with Shakespeare, a subtle though unintentional recognition of the fact that he is as harmless as if he were a classic or dead.

I am, personally, in favour of this impartially neutral British attitude towards the men with ideas: as I said to begin with, it seems to be the secret of much of our present comfort. It does not follow that the man in the street, or I with him, object to ideas as such. We acknowledge them to be the vehicles of human progress. But we cannot help noticing, as we see them forging ahead at top speed in our Europe, that they are fearfully bumpy vehicles; nor do they all appear to be going in the same direction. The British official, that much-maligned creature, acts in a muffling capacity: by the sheer force of bland indifference he does, we admit, slow down the pace of our progressive chariot, but he provides it with springs over the worst jolts. (Springs, appearing to yield and never doing so, are a good simile for the perfect official.)

*   *   *   *   *

Let us reflect for a moment on what would follow if, for one week only, all the letters in *The Times* and *The New Statesman* were taken seriously and put into effect. And let us reflect that something like this actually does happen in many countries. It is not the letters, of course, that get put into effect, since few nations have an actual hand in the manufacture of that 'wise and watchful press' which, according to Eothen, 'presides over the formation of our opinions and brings about this splendid result, namely, that in matters of belief the humblest of us are lifted up to the level of the most sagacious.' But if it is not the letters, it is the sort of people who write them who, instead of being confined, as with us, to

> That strip of Verbiage strewn
> That just divides the Chaos from the Known,

are given a free hand. They have conspired, though usually not with love; they have grasped the sorry scheme of things entire; and having done much of the shattering, are now presumably busy with the remoulding: but what an uncomfortable business.

For one thing, when the men of ideas get busy with progress you can only have one sort of progress at a time. Your real progressives are never fair: they are never sufficiently neutral. We do not watch them willingly and politely handing each other the tiller week and week about. Therefore, while we see one sort of progress rampant in every intellectual country, we know that all the other sorts are there in a suppressed state of fury, kept down only by a mixture of advertisement and force. It is only in England that, simultaneously, every sort has a run for its money – a toddle rather than a run perhaps, but sufficient to keep it in health and humour: and this is due entirely to the fact that the men with ideas are kept in their proper places, below the level of invidious discrimination.

Having got so far in my inquiry, I stumbled with a dazzled surprise on the second, equally efficient but hitherto unsuspected, *raison d'être* of our (comparative) immunity from ills at this present moment. It is partly caused by the segregation of our intelligentsia from the serious side of English public life; but it is also due to the fact that the unpretentious people who *do* run this country sometimes, unexpectedly, develop an idea of their own.

*   *   *   *   *

When querulous highbrows say, as they frequently do, that our public men never think, the statement should not be taken any more seriously than any other of their statements. Serious men in England are bored by the process of thinking and rarely pursue it with passionate, disastrous continental eagerness. But this is from disinclination and not from inability, and the difference is important. When an emergency arises (or perhaps a little after) and someone sits down in an office and thinks from Monday morning to Friday night, the results are remarkable, surprise being the chief element in any sort of contest; the surprise caused by our sudden streaks of imagination is something to which the foreign world has never yet got accustomed. The reason, of course, is that on the Continent people still insist on attending to what our intelligentsia has to say about the government of England.

I imagine that one of the most important political ideas newly developed within the last thirty years is that of government by mandate. At one blow it substituted a new method of growth for the old imperialism based on possession merely. The independence of Iraq, Egypt and Syria, and the federation of India are first fruits of this mighty seed; the fact that the Italian war in Abyssinia, based on imperial ideas of fifty years ago, is now generally felt to be an anachronism is largely due to the new outlook which the system of mandates embodies – the principle that the mainspring of government is not to dominate but to benefit the governed.

But who first thought of mandates? There was a controversy about it some years ago and no one knew precisely. They were, it seems, an English invention, apparently evolved among the typewriters in some office at the time of the Peace Conference or a little earlier. They seem to have come nameless into the world, one of those stepping-stones of unrecognized endeavour, very characteristic of the growth of our Empire.

And now that this unpopular word is out, I come to a point of real controversy with the highbrows.

Why is it that to so many of them the British Empire seems still to be the creature of blood and iron which their grandfathers, young Liberals of a bygone century, used to denounce? Our intelligentsia, whose job it should be to stand above our heads and look horizonwards for passwords of the future, have let themselves be enslaved by old catchwords as miserably as if they were readers of the Beaverbrook Press; they say what their fathers said before them; and one of the greatest revolutions of these decades – less spectacular, but probably far more durable than most others – is coming about unnoticed under their eyes.

What nearly everyone is out for now is 'collective security' and 'the League of Nations'; it is the cry of the day, an excellent cry. But how many realize that collective security and the League of Nations *are* the British Empire today? Leaving the question of Palestine on one side – a tangled business started at the moment when, contrary to our tradition, we allowed a philosopher to be active in politics – leaving this aside, the freedom of small nations at the moment is on the whole safer within than without the Empire.

Our intellectuals, while they are clamouring for collective security *outside,* are frequently careless and sometimes actively against it *inside* the Empire, where it would be so much less complicated to put in practice. The same person who is ardent for intervention in Spain, will talk composedly of handing over slices of Africa or of sitting by while Egypt is annexed by some expansionist. Reasoning with the mind of his grandfather, he still considers it a sign of a liberal education to be willing to give away our possessions. If he knew the territories he talks about, he would realize that there is nothing they fear more or desire less than to be handed over to X or Y, nothing they pray for more earnestly than a clear certainty of protection.

How can we talk of collective security for the world when we tolerate the thought that even the smallest and weakest of those dependent upon us, for whom we have once undertaken responsibility, may be abandoned against their will? The principle is one and the same; our obligations here are closer than those which bind us to the League of Nations, *but of the same kind;* the role of little Englander at present is not that of a noble and altruistic giver, but rather resembles the Russian mother in the sledge who threw one child after another to the wolves.

*   *   *   *   *

It would be pleasant to see a young imperialism awakening in this land: one that, discarding the outworn use of words, could penetrate through the discord of Diehard or Socialist partisans, echoes of yesterday's voices, to the new shape of a reality which already exists. They would know with pride and awe that the *freedom* of many different peoples is in their hands, to be increased in gradual measure until it reaches completion, and to be guarded as their own.

At present an Indian, or an Arab, or a Maltese is an alien in the eyes of most Englishmen in his own he is a member of the British Empire; when he does not feel so, it is indeed our fault. His point of view seems to me more international than ours. He can conceive of a community on something larger than a racial basis. To foster this feeling is to encourage the sort of attitude which alone can produce a League of Nations; to snub it, as we too often do, is to leave a blank which is only filled by an aggressive sort of nationalism, the world's most present curse.

So seen as a community, the British Empire is no enemy to a greater League of Nations, rather a rallying-point for all lesser and weaker seekers after peace; and as for collective security, it will not suffer in this world if, like charity, it begins at home.

1936

A story remembered with tenderness under the cloud of war.

Himyar, the Lizard

Travelling once through sandy, empty regions towards the coast, some two hundred miles east of Aden, one of the half-naked bedouin in our caravan produced a desert lizard from his loin-cloth. He had the little reptile, swollen and rigid with fright, rolled in blue indigo cotton round his waist, and in a halt among the thorn-bushes pulled it out and began to throw it about like a toy, and pounce on its terrified small efforts at escape.

I saved the lizard from these torments, and it became recognized as my property, still carried by its bedu in the darkness of the waistband, but not played with; and when we reached the sea, I found a box for it to creep into, and carried it by dhow to Aden. Here it was to be released among rocks and bushes, but I developed a fever and had no chance to leave Aden town before the sailing of my P. & O. So the lizard travelled with me, no longer swollen and actively defensive, but still petrified and unsociable, and suicidally resolved to starve.

Sympathetic stewards offered everything, from flies to lettuce and lemons, and a small crowd gathered every day to watch it from the cabin door. The lizard crouched like a small crocodile in the darkest corner, pushed its nose against the wall, and stayed there motionless, thinking thoughts of captivity and refusing to be lionized.

By this time I had become attached to it. I called it Himyar, because of the tribe and the hills it came from, and watched anxiously for any diminution in the food with which it was left in tactful solitude. For three weeks the little creature lived on air. He was only thirteen inches long, and when warm and happy had a mottled sand-coloured complexion, something like the rough sandstone of his deserts. But in those early days he showed only a dark greenish tint, signifying – I learned later – fear or worry. He had a spiky tail, as long almost as all the rest of his body, a delicate piece of workmanship made up, I once counted, of a hundred and twenty-one pieces that allowed it to lift or swing in any direction. Perhaps nature intended it to alarm small enemies of the desert, but this was bluff, for Himyar really had no defences at all: his teeth were two long blunt ridges that could bite nothing tougher than a lettuce, and his only threat, that of swelling himself out to thrice his natural size, made him, you would imagine, only more appetizing to birds of prey likely to pounce upon him from the air.

He knew this, as I soon discovered, for when we reached Cairo I stayed in a house with a garden and hired a small Egyptian boy to watch over Himyar, secured from flight by a knotted string around his tail, but otherwise free to ramble. In the sun and among moving leaves he woke to life, though the mystery of the constraining cord harassed him and led him to knot himself tight in wild dashes, terrified by my releasing fingers. One afternoon, however, I found him not moving: he lay flattened, shrunk to his smallest size against the ground, while a black and grey crow, taking its time as if to increase the horror, danced from one foot to the other with outspread wings upon the roof above. The little Egyptian boy, the protector, watching Himyar with a slow accumulation of superstitious fears, had suddenly felt he could bear him no longer, and had fled, and I was only just in time to save him.

Himyar, though he did not know it, was doing the Grand Tour: Egypt, Greece, and Italy were on his programme. He flew with me from Alexandria to Athens, and there spent three weeks, partly in my hotel bedroom, where he now ventured to eat lettuce when alone; and partly running up and down the Acropolis in his little harness, distracting tourists from the things they were intended to admire.

At this stage. Himyar connected me with walks and ceased to be actively afraid. I carried him in the flap of my coat, where he could feel safe in the darkness; and he visited the most illustrious sites of Ancient Greece, including Delphi, where we nearly lost him close to the hole in the ground whence once the Sibyl spoke.

Here Himyar, revelling in grass undreamt of in Arabia, inserted himself between two rocks; when I pulled at his string, it broke. He thought he was free. He reverted, as we do in such moments, to the millennial instincts that precede the Age of Reason. Stuck in his crevice, he swelled so as to fill it from side to side, and Jock Murray and I, blocking the two opposite openings, could only reach him with ineffectual finger-tips that made him bulge out more and more like a dragon in the dim twilight of his refuge. Hours passed. Jock, who had come to spend one happy restful week-end in Greece, made tentative suggestions of defeat, but recognizing female obstinacy in my voice, with instinctive tact withdrew the unworthy words almost before they were uttered. It looked as if we should have to wait until the misguided Himyar once more shrank to normal. A visiting Athenian girls' school, deflected from the glories of their past, grouped themselves about us and started a sort of Chorus on Himyar, strophe and antistrophe.

At last archaeology came to the rescue. A man strolled by with a long metal hook used in restorations of the temple of Apollo just above. This hook Jock inserted with coldly anti-lizard firmness under the little bit of string that still encircled Himyar's tail, and with a lacerating movement dragged him from the sibylline darkness. It is a strange thing how the feeling of responsibility awakens human affection: I felt I could not leave the little creature I had brought from its deserts; and as he slowly shrank and subsided in the friendly darkness of my coat, a bond grew up between us. A week or so later, steaming up the Adriatic, Himyar began to eat his lettuce calmly, sitting on my lap.

* * * * *

My home was on a sunny slope of the hills that surround the Venetian plain and here we made Himyar a good-sized wire cage to run about in. He spent his nights on a hot-water bottle, with a cushion to cover him at the foot of my bed. There he lay torpid, pleased now to be handled. But when the day began to warm his cage, he would become lighter and lighter in colour, and slimmer and gayer, and his little body would grow warm through and through in the life-giving sun. He would climb to welcome me and the walk that was heralded by my coming, and tumble himself out of my hands to trace a regular unaltering itinerary through the garden, which he had come to know. He ran along the brick paths, with a sniff at the flowers that hung over them, swinging their new-opened shadows over his small triangular head – things like roses and carnations, for whose hard petals he had little use; but when he had crossed the rose-pergola and came to an area of grass and clover, he began to dart about in a busy way, and snapped up the honey-sweet heads with greed. He then waddled to some raised beds where the marigolds attracted him; here he pottered about, enjoying the warm brick of the border and ignoring, as if they did not exist, the slick Italian lizards that panted round about him, or the ants that ran their busy caravans among the seeds. Then, suddenly, he would remember, and waddle busily to the lawn, where a feast of dandelions waited; these too he snapped up with the obvious eagerness of the desert where good food is scarce.

After this, a close watch had to be kept, for he returned by a path with a hedge that appealed to truant instincts. He was not made for speed – his quickest waddle was unequal to a fast walk, but he once escaped and was found three days later by some children, a mile and a half away across a valley and a stream; he had been so tame that a peasant had stopped to play with him on the way, but some shock came with the children, and it took me weeks to coax him back to his trust and gaiety. This set-back was painful as cruelty to witness, for there is, in truth, something incredibly appealing in the trust of a wild creature and not for any price would one see it abused. Himyar would now eat out of our hands, waiting with his little three-cornered black eyes twinkling contentedly while dandelions were offered for decapitation. He would play, tossing his head when stroked under the chin; and for me alone he kept a strange and rather alarming sign of affection. His eyes would suddenly grow big and bulgy and turn right round in their sockets, so that at first I thought he was suffering from fits; but as this only happened when he seemed well and happy, and when I stroked the top of his head, I came to the conclusion that it was pure affection, however peculiar in expression.

One could not help admiring the gallantry of the little creature that met and faced so many new things and absorbed them into its life. The flowers that he nibbled with such decided choice can never have been met before on the stony steppe he came from. The stream he crossed must have been a terrifying novelty, and when afterwards I tried giving him warm baths, I found that this experiment also he accepted with pleasure and composure. Fire he had never seen before, and he tried, fascinated, to throw himself bodily into its glow and warmth, until I let one paw touch an ember to show him what it was; he never went too near again.

But fear, mere craven fear, was not in him, and it was a touching sight to see the little lizard crouch, still and wary, flat along the ground, while the daily aeroplane from Venice zoomed overhead, confident in the power of his small strategy against the wings of destiny above. He had inherited certain things, a code one cannot help calling it, of character and conduct. His personal habits were clean and tidy. He had so great a universe against him and so little strength of defence, and for a time, in the summer, even what he had forsook him, for his claws fell off, leaving soft stumps that took some weeks to grow anew. But by this time he knew his friends, and if anything startled him it was enough for me to hold him in my hand for his body to settle back into security and ease. I was filled with a constant wonder that a creature so small and so different, whose very blood was warmed by other laws than ours, should yet share these basic things – affection, trust, and an incredible perseverance and courage. It gave a kindly Franciscan sense of brotherhood, and I could not help reflecting that the distance between ourselves and the infinite wisdom is probably greater than that which separates us from the small lizard-creatures of our world.

However this may be, Himyar wound himself about our hearts, and when, in the autumn of 1938, the Munich crisis packed me off to England at two hours' notice, Himyar was slid under my jacket with a last bunch of dandelions and clover to keep us on our way.

It was a strange journey, the basking autumn land so golden as we left it, the Simplon train so packed with anxious feelings and travellers,

The Zodiac Arch

most of whom the French mercilessly rejected at their frontier. Himyar and I sailed triumphantly through on a British passport, regardless of the fact, which I only discovered in Paris, that it was my mother's passport taken by mistake. But Paris was a desperate city, not concerned with details. No preparation for air-raid defence was visible; a dull silence — determination we thought it then, but it may have been inertia — hung over it like a coma, pierced by the frenzied activities of foreign women trying to get away.

The newspaper headlines spoke of Earl Baldwin, in the House of Lords, in tears. Appalled at the way in which we seemed to be facing our troubles, in a dreary hotel bedroom filled with complicated furniture and marble surfaces, I fed Himyar nostalgically on the flowers of my garden. We reached London safely (still on my mother's passport) and settled down in wondering dismay to 'peace in our time'.

Himyar went with me to one or two week-end parties, where he was the centre of interest, and little parcels of dandelions and clover came for him from the country while the autumn lasted. But the cold was closing in and the problems of feeding and heating grew acute together. The Zoo said mealy-worms: I found this revolting food at Selfridge's, and Himyar refused to give it even the sniff of curiosity he kept for new flowers. But he took to Parma violets, which cost me a shilling a day.

The winter of 1938 was icy, it may be remembered. I padded Himyar's cage with hot-water bottles; a strong electric bulb warmed and lit it; but nothing, I was told later, can take the place of sunlight. Himyar grew thinner and thinner. He still played with me when I came home and my heart was strangely heavy for a creature so remote and so small. One day he made up his mind that the trouble of living was greater than its worth. He turned from his violets; when I coaxed him, he would bend his head, sniff at them, and look away; and in a week or two, a drowsy little crocodile skeleton, he died.

I wept for him. Even now a tightness comes to my throat when I think of Himyar, and remorse for the taking of him so far from the things he knew. The whole cataclysm of our world has swept him away. But there is an appeal in courage which perhaps goes deeper than the roots of man. His was a tiny flame; yet it burned in the face of all that the Unknown presented; and when life was no longer what he cared for, with unwavering certainty he laid it aside. There have been many occasions in the last few years when looking into the face of darkness, I have remembered my little lizard of the rocks.

1944

In the ten years of war which have spread their desolation through my life I can see, as I look back, that the magic and the strength of words, spoken or read or written, was ever my chief refuge – a private impregnable fortress, a cup of safety where the waters of life and love still kept their rainbow reflections and promises of peace. In the last war it was my fortune to deal with words. I came to realize as never before their immense depth and therefore their power, as of the human tool that can, in the end, conquer all things alone. I found in them that secret of the exploring spirit which has been my pleasure since childhood and which is equally at home in action and in thought; and because of this similarity, I have grouped the following essays together in spite of their different dates, since they deal with the sister subjects of Discovery and Style.

A Note on Style

S tyle is something peculiar to one person; it expresses one personality and one only; it cannot be shared. There are as many different styles in the world as there are human beings. They may express themselves in art, in writing, in music, in speech, in dress, in morals, in life. I will illustrate this by taking the easiest example – of style in dress. A woman may wear the most expensive clothes – if they are bought without sense and taste, they will be just clothes, they will not express the wearer's own personality, they will have no style. It is the same with the conduct of life in general: if you take your thoughts and your principles from other people or books, without making them your own, without digesting them with thought and feeling, you become a mere weak echo of other voices – your life has no style. In literature it is exactly the same: if you use beautiful words to express thoughts that are not your own thoughts – echoes meaningless because borrowed from other people – you have no personality and no style. The advice for a good style is very simple: you must first have something you want to say and then you must say it. But it must be what *you* want to say. That is why I put courage as the first virtue for style; the courage of one's own belief.

The second virtue is accuracy or truth. Whatever it is you may want to say, you must try to say it as exactly as you can. You must not be led astray by words, by emotions, by vague echoes, to say things you do not mean. This sounds easy, but very few people attain to such simple truth. When, for instance, you write 'a mountain is beautiful' you are not really speaking the truth about the mountain, you are saying nothing at all, for the idea of beauty is a vague idea in your mind, it gives no accurate picture of the mountain you wish to describe. You must look at your mountain, its shape, its height, its atmosphere, the trees that clothe it, the clouds that visit it, its remoteness, its history, a hundred things about it, and see them all in their proper places and relations to each other, and when you have hunted and found words for all these things, you must condense them to the small size you require, and express all these hundred meanings in a handful of words. Then perhaps you can say in two single lines what Coleridge said about Mont Blanc:

> Oh struggling with the darkness all the night,
> And visited all night by troops of stars.

In these words he has condensed all he has seen, he has given the height of the mountain, its strength, its remoteness and permanence under the changing heavens: he has observed, and chosen what was most significant. That is what I mean by truth.

The two virtues, of courage and truth, if you understand them and apply them to your writing, will of themselves give you an honourable style, at any rate in prose. But there is another important quality which applies to the sound, as distinct from the sense, of words. This is a quality which human beings share with animals. The style of a cat when angry and spitting is quite different from when it is purring and happy; it manages to express feeling by sound alone. A good writer can also do this to a great extent. You would never for instance use soft and gentle words like evening, lovely, amethyst, melody, to express rage or fear or anything violent. I do not myself know why some words are gentle while others are violent and harsh; perhaps it goes very far back in the history of mankind, and the soft letters are those like the vowels, or 'l' and 'v', which one pronounces with the lips relaxed and half open while the hard sounds are those you might utter under great stress or pain; at any rate the sound of words can be used to give richness and variety to the meaning of what you say, and poets especially use this melody of language to good purpose.

> The quality of mercy is not strained,
> It droppeth as the gentle rain from heaven . . .

If you say the same thing in other words you get a different (a regrettably different) effect:

> The attribute of compassion is effortless
> It descends from the sky like rain.

Eyen the moving of a single word from one place to another can make or ruin a whole line: for instance, when Lycidas 'Sleeps by the fable of Bellerus old', you ruin the whole thing if you say 'sleeps by the fable of old Bellerus' though the sense remains exactly the same. It is quite interesting to take any fine author and to try to substitute some of the words he uses, and to see how and why his style is weakened when you do so. You will find that the greatest writers have nearly always found the *only* word; anything you can put instead is incomplete.

I have now given what are, I believe, the three chief qualities in style; courage in what you say, truth in your manner of saying it, and that mysterious harmony of words which can only be trained as an ear is trained in music. To all this one must add something for the *importance* of style. You will realize it when you consider that the only foundation for good writing is good thinking; and when we think well, we act well; the question of style is therefore bound up both with our thoughts and our deeds. That is why the great ages of nations are also the great ages of their literature; their words come out of their thoughts and acts, and in their turn inspire them. I have often been impressed by the peculiar nobility of language of the Arabs of the desert, and I think it comes largely from their life of freedom and of danger. An old friend of mine, years ago, was ship-wrecked with Wilfred Blunt in a pilgrim ship off Tor on the Red Sea. They were stranded on a reef, beaten by the waves, and with some difficulty were able to send an Arab ashore to go for help to Tor; there he sent a telegram for a gunboat to come and rescue them. But when the postmaster at Tor asked him to pay for the telegram, the man replied scornfully: 'What should I know of money, who come from death and the sea?' That is a good example of style.

1942

Exploring with Words

There was a wise man in China who had travelled in his youth, until he found that he learnt more and went further in the leisure of his garden, and it would be hard to say whether he was more of an adventurer during the first or the second sort of journey. It is indeed a most difficult matter to decide who is and who is not an explorer and I am inclined to think the secret of all exploration the same – a wish to grasp a little more fully the universe in which we live. Perhaps the physical explorer, the traveller from land to land, is of a rather inferior kind: a person who needs a gross and obvious stimulus and cannot make his own universe walking like Plato 'in the groves of the academy'. I remember seeing, along a suburban road when I was fourteen or fifteen years old, a little semi-detached house with the name 'The Odyssey' written up on its small gateway and being reproached by my mother for laughing at it, because surely, she said, a name like that was written by someone who had his dreams and must have been an explorer at heart.

If, then, we refuse to limit ourselves to people who actually travel, we must find characteristics of a basic nature in exploration. I can think of three. The first is one that deals with it in its relation to other human beings; and there the great advantage is the teaching of toleration. This is the hall-mark of all true explorers and by no means of the ordinary traveller, of whom the saying that 'travel broadens the mind' is very common and most untrue. In fact I think that the explorer will have his mind broadened by whatever his occupation may be, while the non-explorer is hardened and congealed in a fanatical sort of ignorance the more he is taken away from the familiar things in which he feels his spiritual safety to lie. The only way in which travel broadens the mind is that, by taking people into new surroundings, it may suddenly reveal the explorer to himself.

Of course a variety of experience is bound to place your own particular universe on a wider basis. I was brought up in a very wandering sort of way with a childhood spent about equally in England, in Italy and in France, and can remember how strange it seemed to me to find people secure in their separate traditions and equally sure that only their own were right. This feeling has never left me; and sometimes in some drawing-room where only one code is admitted, I think of remote tribes and places where, with such different manners and surroundings, the same certainty of lightness prevails.

The true explorer is rarely sure that he is right – and never sure that he is right alone. When an Italian ecclesiastic invited the Qadhi of Tripoli to dinner, the Muslim dignitary was offered ham at repeated intervals; he refused and refused and at last explained that it was forbidden by his religion. 'You don't know what a pleasure you miss', said his host. When the guest rose to leave, he thanked the monsignor for his hospitality and begged him to thank his wife also for the excellent meal which she had, no doubt, prepared. The Italian churchman explained that he could have no wife: it was forbidden by his religion. 'Alas,' said the Qadhi, 'you don't know what a pleasure you miss.' Such is the barrier. But in 1609 John Jourdain, a Dorset man, described his arrival in Perim where he visited the tomb of a prophet and said as he went on his way, 'I let him sleep with God or the devil, not knowing whose servant he is.' That is the sensible exploring point of view, and you will find it in all the great travellers – in Froissart, Herodotus, in the great Arabs, and in our own. In Christopher Sykes's sketch of Robert Byron the point is made: he had 'studied Europe from Greece, England from India, Byzantium from Russia, Persia from China and Europe again from the United States' – he had learnt toleration.

This first gift of exploration deals with other people; the second, with ourselves. The great aim of exploration, its real and deepest advantage, the best reason and justification for it, is that it gives us a sense of values; whether his journey be along the shelves of his library or the deserts of Asia, the explorer should come out with a philosophy of his own at the end of it. The accidental and the enduring separate themselves and come to be distinguished. And this, at any rate to me, is the great and ever-renewed joy of travel; that one finds the things that are permanent among all sorts of human beings in every race of men. Perhaps women have an advantage in this respect, because our interests are anyway basic and universal; children, clothes, and food; these are really the same in every quarter of the world and will be important when all political parties are forgotten. In fact the ordinary life of a woman is in itself an exploration in a way that the civilized man's life has ceased necessarily to be, for the bearing of children brings even the most humdrum woman face to face with the unknown. But men, too, indeed all of us together, have an exploration to make and we may find it useful to have learnt gaiety and endurance, curiosity and delight to help us venture into the unknown when it comes. *The Pilgrim's Progress* must ever be the firmest textbook and the best excuse for exploration.

The artist who creates is also led into the wilderness that surrounds us. The things that are current there are current throughout the whole human race and perhaps beyond it; and to discover them means a discovery of the real brotherhood of man. Mr Ellis Roberts makes this point very clear in a comparison between Richard Burton and Charles Doughty:

'The instinct to imitate, to cloak your own convictions and to follow alien and perhaps disliked conventions, is based on a deep distrust of human brotherhood. The man who really believes that the distinctions of race, colour, language and creed are ultimately less important than the fact of our common humanity is never afraid to admit the reality and significance of these distinctions: the man who minimizes the reality of the distinctions in the human family is the man who, at bottom, suspects them of having a terribly potent force, a force stronger than that of the brotherhood which is human nature's indefeasible privilege.

'Doughty never leaves us with the impression that he is investigating some strange half-human society; his contact is direct, sincere, instinctive, just because the point of view is remote and separate. He is painting a picture of people like himself who happen to have different habits and a different creed.'

I only came upon this quotation the other day but it is a thing I have often noticed on my own account and have explained over and over again to people living their own strange lives; and I have always found that they discovered with a great delight this common basis of humanity beneath our different habits. In a very dangerous and fanatical country it is advisable to make this a text for one's conversation over and over again. Villages that are reluctant to see strangers using their cups and plates can gradually be brought to realize that there is a sort of harmony, universal and fundamental, beneath the discords of history and custom and belief.

In the literary world, the exploring mind alone can hold the key of style (not that it always does so). The chief ingredient is truthfulness, the sort of truthfulness one tries for in a telegram, to give an unambiguous message in essential words. An ear for the rhythm and music of sentences must be added; but truthfulness is the main, and this – a disinterested wish for direct vision – is the explorer's gift, and even the rhythm has a part in truthfulness. When you say 'green is the valley' you are not saying that 'the valley is green'; the difference in position and emphasis has made a different picture, and the person who is anxious to give an accurate account of what is in his mind will not be free to choose one or the other at random. The explorer is not a person who, like the tourist, sets out with a set of ideas he is not anxious to alter; he goes out to collect raw material for his life – for something he is making which had not taken shape before.

In his effort to express this, his language or art becomes a means and not an end and acquires style in direct relation to the truthfulness which he is able to attain. What I may call the magic of style is in direct proportion to the depth of truthfulness, to the layer, as it were, of reality which it reaches. In Shakespeare one can often see this immense and passionate vision pierce right through and almost split the capacity of words to carry it; and I would like to give you an example or two to show the degrees by which this passion is reached: first from the wild geese in *A Midsummer Night's Dream* who

> Rising and cawing at the gun's report,
> Sever themselves and madly sweep the sky.

This is a piece of honest accurate observation.
And next:

> . . . the eastern gate, all fiery red,
> Opening on Neptune with fair blessed beams,
> Turns into yellow gold his salt green streams.

This is also a concise, accurate description, with 'Neptune' the only fancy word, but the beginning of magic with the ripple of movement through the colour, a thing not static but alive – the words 'opening', 'turns', 'streams', are all words that have movement and a developing sort of movement, like the growth of the light penetrating these colours. But here in *Anthony and Cleopatra* comes the great magic:

> . . . This common body,
> Like to a vagabond flag upon the stream,
> Goes to and back, lackeying the varying tide,
> To rot itself with motion.

The vision, just as accurate and telegraphically concise, reaches a deeper layer where the essence of the crowd and the water-weed are identical – and in this depth the magic is born. It is tremendous in a fourth example:

> And there is nothing left remarkable
> Beneath the visiting moon.

Movement and space and cold, a derelict world, are gathered into this wonderful verb: but it is all the same principle of observation in depth, of an exploring mind making its own impact upon reality, which is a synonym of the unknown – and creates style.

There is a third benefit of exploration that belongs more to the physical than to the mental explorer, and that is the general mastery obtained over oneself by the custom and disregard of hardships unavoidable, but with differences between them. It seems to me that the essence of the matter is whether they are voluntary or involuntary. To be given a cold bath is not a merit in itself; to take one voluntarily is quite a different matter. I would like to quote again from Mr Sykes's book where he speaks of a man who came serene and fortified out of the horrors of a German prison camp.

> 'He resisted torture [he said] by offering it to God, but to maintain the personal nature of his penance he added to his pain; thus when obliged to sleep in a cell without bed or blanket he deprived himself of his coat also; when whipped or submitted to other pain he would afterwards lie on stones, or he would inflict additional pain on himself with his nails or teeth. . . . He had no childish intention of presenting a voracious God of sacrifices with a bumper record of anguish undergone. He followed this system, he said, simply to preserve a sense of his own personality.'

The explorer deals with the vicissitudes of life in rather the same spirit. He says, 'I'm going to trample on myself and what is more I am going to do it for fun!' This in its measure is a triumph over life and death and time. And that it is so is shown by the fact that in spite of all hardships, discomforts and sicknesses the lure of exploration still continues to be one of the strongest lode-stars of the human spirit, and will be so while there is the rim of an unknown horizon in this world or the next.

1947

Travel for Solitude

It is usually assumed that the traveller who prefers lonely places – the desert traveller, so to say – is one who wishes to escape from his world and his fellows. The popular conception gives to his wanderings a touch of misanthropy. To him the gentle things of every day make no appeal; the intercourse of humanity – that fragile house of cards built with such delicate and assiduous labour through millenniums of time, threatened by every cataclysm, and which yet stands because of the mere fact that every card leans up against the other – this finite and infinite structure of civilization is supposed to be the object of his aversion, the atmosphere from which he turns away.

I should like to offer a far less negative interpretation of the longing which leads men out into the wastes. The Lord Byrons of this world,

> Tired of home, of wife, of children tired
> The restless spirit is driven abroad to roam,

are rather bogus spirits more often than not. I have a suspicion that Lord Byron himself might easily have settled into a domesticated middle age if his fates had not cut the thread so soon. The discontented are the least capable of all people to live with themselves for very long; and the same goad which has driven them out into the wilderness will prick them home again.

The true wanderer, whose travels are happiness, goes out not to shun, but to seek. Like the painter standing at his easel, he moves constantly to get his perspective right, and feels, though half a country may be spread out to a far horizon in his view, that he is too close to his picture and must get away now and then to look at it with an eye of distance. This necessity keeps him for ever on his feet. He touches and retouches the tones of his world as he sees them; and it is to make the proportions more accurate that he travels away from them, to come back with a more seeing and a rested eye.

It is, of course, absurd to think that one gets away from the world by moving into lonely places. All that happens is that one reaches a simplified world, with few personal attachments of one's own. The human figure itself takes on immense majesty when you meet it solitary in a landscape that scarcely speaks of humanity at all – where no fields, no walls, no hedges, no milestones, telegraph-poles and unnaturally straight lines of road make the single human being seem less important by adding continuity to the image of humanity as a whole. Ruins go well with deserts for this reason; the human continuity is visibly broken by them, and the rare human figures you may meet among them stand doubly isolated in space and time. Even without ruins or deserts, the sea or the mountains can create the same impression, of dignity and gallantry, round the fisherman's boat aslant in the trough of the waves, or the shepherd with his flock, alone on pastoral edges where the high rocks come down. The smallness and the weakness of the human creature is there made unmistakably apparent, and yet at the same time you feel in yourself the elation of victory, the knowledge that the solitary, puny being is the master of his immense horizon; and if you yourself are sharing the life of solitude and hardship, you feel that you too have a part in the victory which you see.

This is a true feeling, presenting humanity as it is, amid the antiquity, the size and grandeur of earth. It is worth a long hard journey to attain it, for it is scarcely to be found in towns or easy places, where men triumph so habitually one over the other that their more cosmic victories are difficult to distinguish. For every victory of man over man has in itself a taste of defeat, a flavour of death; there is no essential difference between the various human groups, creatures whose bones and brains and members are the same; and every damage we do there is a form of mutilation, as if the fingers of the left hand were to be cut off by the right; there is no pleasure in it, nor any deep sense of achievement or of peace.

We like the country, and even more so the comparatively, desert places, because there we can take pleasure in watching with far less interruption the progress and the triumphs of mankind. The countryman is not, I imagine, nobler than his fellows, nor is the sympathy that we, travellers in Arabia, feel for the rough bedouin a result of any marked superiority of theirs over other men. Their violence, their crimes against their own kind and therefore against themselves, are, if anything, greater than the average that our civilization allows; and yet we are happy because we can see behind these crimes a background of real and vast achievement, the primitive vanquished background of Earth. The courtesy of the desert Arab who stands in his poor tent to receive the stranger is not greater necessarily than that of the diplomat at the head of his staircase; yet a difference is made by the darkness of the surrounding hills, by the stony hardness of their paths, by the scarcity of food and water. Even the smallest crumb of grace or virtue is a triumph when the whole darkness of earth and time lies around it; and we are constantly comforted even for the worst crimes in those lands of treachery and murder by the sight of a victory immeasurably greater than these defeats, wrested by the whole of humanity out of the 'fell clutch of circumstance.'

This is, I believe, the obscure reason which has lured not only explorers, but hermits, saints and philosophers into their solitudes. They are not anxious to leave the paths of their fellows, but they do seek the less frequented stretches, where – free from obstructions – they can comfort themselves with the certainty that the path does go uphill and not down. It is, of course, not impossible to make sure of the same fact in other surroundings. More discrimination and more imagination are required, and also a mind less sensitive, less alert to the impact of what surrounds it, so that it may keep the essential truth in sight through all the contradictions of times and men. Socrates loved the market-place, and his sense of proportion was not impaired; but perhaps he is not a fair example, for the light of Attica is a very clear light and preferable to most deserts even now. The artist, too, if he is sufficiently in earnest, can follow his vision in a crowd, and is made happy perpetually by the victory of the human spirit, in which he has the delight of taking an active part; and of the scientist, pursuing knowledge for its own sake, the same may be said. But to most even of these, and to many of lesser calibre, it is a help and a rest to get away for a while to where the pattern of mankind is traced in less complicated lines, so that background and direction show clearly beyond the tangle of our self-inflicted sorrows.

I have often noticed that the eyes of sailors and hillmen are free and quiet. Countrymen, too, when they walk among their fields, and women who surround themselves with love in their homes and think rather little of what lies beyond, old men contented with the end of their journey, and painters, carpenters and all makers, when happy in their jobs – these and many others, men and women who have found their true vocations, share the same atmosphere of certainty and peace. I have noticed, too, that the business of these people is never such that it makes them consciously share in the wounding of their fellows, whether through rivalries, or vanities, greed or envy; not only are they free of such impulses in themselves, but the happiness of their condition is such that they are largely exempted from watching this strife in others, either through the solitude of their lives or through the absorbing interest of what they care for. For it is to be hoped, and I think believed, that the worried look visible on so many city faces is more due to the constant witnessing than to the constant infliction of pain – though both must take their share in a competitive life. Those who are happily free from this affliction have no need to travel; they can sit quietly and continue to be philosophers at home.

To the rest of us the roads lie open and lead to a true and happy panorama of our world. We will avoid mere sight-seeing and the rush of trains, or cars, or liners, where the suicidal tendencies of mankind are just as visible as in a street of bankers; and will confine ourselves to two sorts of landscape, each of which can give us what we need by different means. We may go to some quiet land, not over-populated, where there is enough natural prosperity for contentment, enough leisure for beauty, enough poverty for kindness, and enough labour for health – some mountain land like the Dolomites, where the harvests are sufficient to feed the villages, and the families go in summer to cut their hay and live in their wooden chalets high up amid their pastures in the sun. Here one need not search out one man in many hundred with the look of contentment in his eyes; one meets it, clear as the current of the mountain streams, in the glance of almost every passer-by; and that is the human comfort of the hills.

Or one may go to the wilderness where there is no consolation of human peace, but where the magnitude of Nature is so apparent, the reality of her obstacles so visible, that the smallness of our achievements matters no longer. The fierce and tiny tribes can tear and lacerate each other; we see that this is a mere incident in the colossal triumph achieved by man in his mere existence, with whatever small measure of order, courtesy and goodness he has managed to collect. And we are comforted because we know in our hearts that the city and the desert background are the same, and the noise of our machines is not much louder than the tribal battle-cry, and is just as temporary against our tremendous background in space and time.

1950

Saying What One Means

I am asked now and then how a 'Style' is acquired. I am sure I don't know! It is one of those things like a light hand at pastry. All sorts of ingredients must go to make up a product – fundamentally the same and superficially so different for every individual.

One is safe, however, in pointing out a basis without which no respectable style is possible – and this is the capacity to say, more or less, what one means. It is not as easy as it seems. Let anyone who doubts take some simple object – a teapot, a chair, a vegetable – and try to describe it exactly: he will come up at once against the formidable inexactitude of language. It is only when he has succeeded in following Flaubert's advice – to describe a tree so that no other tree could be mistaken for it – it is only then that his stylistic problem will be on its way to be solved.

Colours for instance are extraordinarily difficult. There is a muddy little canal I often pass, and I have puzzled for a week at a time over its colour. It is indeed exactly like putty, but one could not use such a word for any sort of water without instantly destroying the idea of fluidity. The point to remember is that every word calls up far more of a picture than its actual meaning is supposed to do, and the writer has to deal with all these silent associations as well as with the uttered significance. I noticed this once when walking along a street full of beggars in Cairo; they came up asking for alms in the name of Allah and I paid little attention to the too familiar sound: until one said: 'By *God*, I am hungry' – and the word God, which we use forcefully and rarely, immediately compelled me to give.

Comparing our new Bible with the Authorized Version, the passionate wish for exactitude seems to me more noticeable in the old translation than in the new, however their actual achievements may compare. Take a rather clumsy sentence from the old – the third verse in the first chapter of St John: 'All things were made by Him and without Him was not any thing made that was made.' Regardless, we may say, of style, the word *thing* together with the insistence on the word *made* do lead the hearer or reader to realize the deadness of matter before a living divinity inspires it. The modern version reads: 'and through him all things *came to be*' (as if it could be an accident!); 'no single thing was created without him' (and why *single?* It might be double, treble or infinite). The old wording '*not any thing made that was made*' is far stronger.

Take also – in the same chapter of the modern version: 'When all things began, the Word already was'. The point is that *things* didn't *begin,* they *were begun*: the old and beautiful opening does not lose sight of this context. 'In the beginning was the word': it concentrates on the main fact and is supremely fitting.

Accuracy is indeed the basis of style. Words dress our thoughts and should fit; and should fit not only in their utterances, but in their implications, their sequences, and their silences, just as in architecture the empty spaces are as important as those that are filled. The problem of all writing is the same as that presented by the composition of a telegram: one has to convey a meaning with the use of few and always inadequate words, and eke it out with what the reader, drawing upon his own reserves, will understand. The number of words that even the most profuse writer will dare to use is always insufficient for a complete impression, but the reserves that he can draw upon in the reader's mind are lavish indeed. The whole generalship of writing is in the summoning and marshalling of these unseen auxiliaries.

This necessary co-operation makes tradition in literature valuable – the gradual development of a vast familiar field. It also makes it difficult to acquire a 'style' in a foreign language, where the writer must rely on his own words merely and has few or none of the subtleties of his readers' background to play with. It is as if a musician were condemned to have the resonance taken out of his notes.

Even the best stylist fails wherever his appeal finds no echo. The words he uses come down from their embroidered past, and wield their magic in the proportion in which this rich sort of tracery is understood: and even the simple mere beauty of sound is built by an infinity of unrecognized associations. The writer's business is to make all this as intelligible as he can. With sequences not too abrupt, with images not too remote, with necessary pauses, he must think how best to use the few words that are given him to deal with the unmanageable multiplicity of nature, even at her easiest; relying on what echo he is able to awaken in the recesses of his reader's mind.

1963

The following four sketches recollect the landscape of war both north and south.

The coming of war must always be a most shattering human experience, because it deals not with mere circumstance, but with the background of life. As in one of those Renaissance pictures of the victory of the younger gods, we see the helpless struggling Titans staked: the landscape of their world, the rocks and trees and hills, have been piled on top of them and have crushed them; and there, pinned down, Enceladus in Etna, they are helpless under the hostility of all that once existed for their delight and use. It is as if the scenery were suddenly to take command of the actors, and no monstrosity except a tidal wave or an earthquake can compete with this sudden reversal, which we find in the state of war, of all the world's natural amenity. In this onslaught of chaos, the noble creature, man, clings to whatever anchors of fortitude have presumably brought him through the ages, and in the measure of their immortality he finds his solace and his respite.

My Worst Journey: 1943

When I was asked to write about my 'worst journey' I looked back over what is now a varied collection of adventures and was perplexed to find no single one among them that I could consider definitely bad. There are days in every journey when everything goes wrong. To be weatherbound in some snug place unknown to all your friends and even – you may hope – to Destiny itself, is one of the cosiest experiences in the world: but to be caught by weather in the open, or at the wrong moment, or with sickness as an added complication, is as unpleasant as anything external can be. And nearly every journey has some such days or hours. There is in fact almost always a moment when you wonder with amazement why you ever set out at all. You have left your props behind you, all the *furniture* of your life, the barricade of things and people erected by yourself and your forebears against the attacks of circumstance; and circumstance is now all about you, with pin-prick or stiletto as the case may be; and nothing but yourself to pit against it, for even the best of guides or hosts or friends you may have collected are new and unsettled in your ways, and if your own inner power gives out they too are bound to fail. It is, I think, the fear of one's own exhaustion that makes the bad moment of the journey – with the knowledge that nothing is there to supplement your own resources if they give way.

In these moments, the best thing to do if one can is to sleep. When I was a child, I used to think of my bed as an island of safety; the dangerous shadows that lurked – especially around the corners of the bedroom – were there, by some mysterious power, kept at bay; and my camp-bed has retained this sort of magic, and often receives me in a short neutrality of peace when chaos threatens all around.

But there is one place where even this refuge fails and the privacy of one's bunk is merely one more cell in a whole system of misery. This is the Atlantic under what the stewardess will tell you – with that hard brisk cheerful air – is merely 'a bit of a breeze'. One should, I think, be ready to pay for one's pleasures, and I could bear the horror, if the Atlantic in its happier moments seemed to me worth anything at all. But let us face the fact: except in the eyes of a few fanatics (untrustworthy as all lovers) an unmitigated expanse of water is dull even when blue: not in a small boat, where you are a part of the winds and currents and tides and are allowed to hold the tiller now and then; but from those decks which the shipping companies with subconscious insight try to make as suburban as possible so that the impact of the monster outside may be lessened, and where the unrecognized boredom is so deep that a wispy smear of smoke on the horizon will queue up a crowd as if for a Valkyrie passing.

This gives the measure of the Atlantic when kind – and when unkind, who can assess it? I look back over all the bad hours it has given me – its freezing coldness, its instability, its nauseating whiffs of oil from the engine-room and smell of paint in the bathroom, its horrid way of making the bath-water slant, so that one feels that something in the laws of gravity has gone askew; above all its efforts at entertaining, like a virago's smile with no kindness beneath it – deck tennis and sweepstakes for all, and the officers' attentions turned on like switches; until one wonders whether any of the other big fish swimming about around us out of sight carry as much dreariness inside them as we do. Nor is the recipe I am always being given against boredom of any use to me at all. One should study one's fellow passengers, they say: a fatal thing to do if one feels as I always feel on an Atlantic crossing.

I have faced the northern ocean five times and the last time was the worst, and I feel that I can choose it without a runner-up for my worst journey. It was in 1943, the middle of the war, and November. Because I am an optimist in spite of past experience, a faint, doubtful glamour hung about the thought of the convoy gathering in the North, as I rattled up in a pleasantly and unusually warm sleeper from King's Cross. I had been in two convoys twice through the Red Sea, and what with islands in sight, and aeroplanes – some friendly and others not – and warm weather and a boat too small for deck drill, the time had gone pleasantly. And Glasgow gave us one of those soft mild winter days, with an illusion of spring round the corner, with the Clyde lying grey as a kitten curled in mists, the woods of its headlands soft as water, and its open basins pale and bright as sky.

There, in an open but noticeably secret solitude, the convoy was gathered, steamless shapes sheltered from sight by the hills. Out of the special train which took us from Glasgow to our unnamed destination, we were piloted and embarked on the *Aquitania*. A last little halo of luxury surrounded the name in our imagination, as we climbed up the side: and then we were shown our quarters, and illusions vanished.

The ship was 'stripped' of course; she was carrying, we were told, five thousand British troops – to America – to the Pacific beyond – who knows? But there they were, with their hammocks slung deck below deck in view when we went down for meals, in air which – compared to the pleasant openness of a bedouin tent – seemed to me unbreathable, packed so close together that some of them must surely think now and then how a bomb here and there is not so undesirable if it makes a little more room on the planet? They were admirably cheerful, and filled our only saloon with a sort of collective haze, a turmoil in which individuals vanished and only khaki wreathed in tobacco smoke and punctuated with faces seemed to exist with an amorphous, temporary life. Over their heads, cleared now and then by the eddies of the smoke, the *Aquitania's* luxury ceiling appeared and hid itself; and it was this sight of former splendour under the stripping, a gilt bracket, a tattered skirting, a bit of painted doorway gone dark with unwashed touches, that gave us our atmosphere of squalor: a clean bare boarded room would have been clear of this nostalgia of decay.

There were a few women, nearly all with babies, who seemed (by the carefulness of his instructions) to weigh heavily on our captain's mind; at all costs infants are sheltered to grow up for another war. Their pink little faces wrapped in shawls were inured twice a day to deck drill, with kind officers helping mothers to arrange the cork jackets for two. The Atlantic howled by in its usual gruesome and useless hurry, putty-green flecked with white. The seagulls made sudden dips sidewards, their round eyes fixed on food. The day rolled low in the sky from squall to squall. After an hour or so of standing about, thinking perforce of shipwrecks, the fug in the saloon was quite welcome.

A little cabin for one person had been arranged to hold four of us women bound for the U.S.A. Here we could lie on our bunks and read in an atmosphere of friendliness and comparative privacy; for we soon discovered that it is *people* who are the chief bane of the collective life. Our little oasis looked like a slum, with all we needed for six days or seven hung out on various strings; but the heart of it was sound, with great helpfulness and kindness inside it; and its worst irritations were the luxury gadgets made for a single occupant, which uselessly used up valuable room, and the thin threads of icy Atlantic air that seemed, like ghosts, to pass through solid metal, for the darkened porthole was battened down from seven at night to seven in the morning, for fear of submarines.

We were, we soon discovered, not in convoy at all. The *Aquitania* was so big and so strong that she could do better by herself and relied on secrecy and swiftness to get her across. Like a greyhound through grass, she sped day and night with her strong thudding heart, and those dismal Atlantic waves flattened themselves against her, with their sodden possibilities of death inside them. How is it possible, I thought, that people ever cross this detestable ocean for *pleasure?* For three days, morning and afternoon, the siren hooted and we took our cork jackets, that filled up half our cabin, on deck, and the inhabitants of each boat began to form a pattern that recognized itself, and the sea – as we came towards its middle fastnesses – stretched its waves into long wizened sinews and even its foam seemed grey like the storm-clouds above.

On the third or the fourth day out, I cannot remember which, I developed acute appendicitis. I was not told what it was but the pain was so violent that the doctor came, and looked at me with a blank young face of panic inspired, I thought, merely by the awfulness of having to deal with a woman in this world of men – for the ship's hospital was full, and there were no nurses but only orderlies about. The one stewardess, her time already overfull of mothers and babies, looked compassionate but remote. They gave me what I was afterwards told was M. & B., and explained that I had a gastric cold; I was exonerated from boat drill and had the relief of thinking that, if necessary, I could now drown in a quiet independent way by myself. For the next three days I lay in my bunk, fed by kind companions with such few things as are suitable for appendicitis out of the menu of a troopship in war. I had books; and the horizon kept itself quiet below the circle of the porthole: but the weary nights dragged minute by minute in an almost intolerable absence of air, interspersed with icy intervals down the long dim clanking corridors of metal, groaning and straining as they pulled us through the sea. How I longed for seven o'clock and the opening of the porthole, and the sight of the sullen, wind-ripped grey! And lifting myself to look out over the sunless ridges, I tried to remember the existence of the blue Mediterranean, the little journeys from harbour to harbour in ancient grooves, the well-worn Graeco-Roman world. When we berthed in Halifax, late on the fourth evening of my illness, I felt suddenly as if nothing could keep me alive through another night of this captivity; the doctor, increasingly worried, evidently felt about it as I did, and at eleven at night I was tucked up on a stretcher in blankets and lifted down a gangway on to land.

The five thousand troops must have thought that some pampered general was being allowed ashore while they were battened down for another set of hours almost as uncomfortable as mine. Tier above tier up the huge ship's side their dim crowding faces lined the narrow slits of decks as they leaned out with whistles and cat-calls of annoyance; until, in a slanting drizzle, preceded by a small lantern and with four men carrying the stretcher, my small self appeared like the funeral of Sir John Moore at Corunna, surrounded by darkness and rain. A complete silence fell on the five thousand while they looked down and I looked up, and the stretcher bearers stumbled along; and the immense smooth flank of the *Aquitania* seemed to lift itself out of sight into the starless region of the elements where she belonged. But I was now on a pleasantly quiescent cobbled street; lifted into an ambulance;

transported to an infirmary; unwrapped by a kind and soothing nun and put into a four-legged bed with sheets that could tuck in. Little I cared for what happened to me.

When the surgeon came in the morning, I was operated on at two hours' notice and, as the appendix had meanwhile already broken, the chances of success seemed small. But I passed through it all without a hitch, and was walking in a fortnight, and travelling to New York in three weeks or four. This remarkable result, which – I learned afterwards – surprised everyone except myself who knew nothing about it, was due in the first place to the skilled surgery and devoted nursing which I think of with gratitude often; but in the second place I think it was also due to the unsurpassable unpleasantness of the Atlantic, which inspires a philosophic and placid acceptance of any other trial – the best psychological preparation for operations of any kind. And this proves, too, what I wrote at the beginning of this article, that no journey can be called wholly bad or good; since nothing but the monstrous wetness of the Atlantic can inspire that passionate relief and rejoicing in the mere dryness of land when it appears.

1954

The Wise Men

I was once asked, during the war, to write somebody's Christmas speech. It was to be made to troops in Egypt; and I was misguided enough to weave it round the theme that the original and genuine Christmas, far from being snow-bound with candlelight and bright crackling fires, had really closely resembled the sharp snowless nights of the desert, with their silences and stars – what our army, in fact, was then looking at all the time. It was the second winter of the war and – with scanty arms, with terribly unequal numbers – the first great leap into the Western desert was preparing, unknown to all except a very few: Bardia, Sidi Barrani, Benghazi were just round the corner, but still hidden in time: all we could see were the great dangers, the great expanses: and I thought of our men lying like the shepherds on the dark dry ground, but in battle-dress beside their tanks or armoured cars, waiting for their good tidings to come. 'Peace on earth: goodwill towards men': to whom could such a message speak more sharply than to a soldier sleeping out in the desert war?

But my effort was rightly rejected. Snow and candles, I was told, was what the men wanted and historical accuracy was out of place. And Christmas, in fact, is not an external event at all, but a piece of one's home that one carries in one's heart: like a nursery story, its validity rests on exact repetition, so that it comes around every time as the evocation of one's whole life and particularly of the most distant bits of it in childhood.

During the war my Christmases were spent in Luxor, in Baghdad, in London and New York, and in the hinter-land of Aden; and this last is the one that remains most vivid in my mind, not because of the nostalgia with which we celebrated it – in 1939 with all our trials before us, a little company separated by great distances and uncertainties from our homes, in a Government rest-house among high rocky hills – and not even because of the strangeness, the hard medieval beauty of the setting; but because we were there in the lands from which the Three Kings, the Wise Men of the East, traditionally started, the only part of Asia where the frankincense will grow.

This was the Land of Uz, the country of Job, and by riding up a steep hill for some hours one could look across an enormous landscape, water-scooped valleys and wind-sculptured ridges, brown and dark not temporarily through the winter months but with a lined and shrivelled rock-hearted permanent darkness; and there on a high thin ledge, whitewashed and visible from afar, was Job's tomb. In the flat valley-bottoms far below, teased by the shifting torrents as by capricious lovers – now swamping them and now absent altogether – the patch-work fields showed their pathetic meagre hopes, their plots of melon or thin rows of millet and maize; and the peasants, dressed in dark blue cotton, wound down to them from tiny villages in strong places, tumbled together out of rocks like the hills that built them, by paths too steep to keep straight, zig-zagging down huge shoulders.

In this country, tradition placed the unknown star and the men who had the wisdom to see it and to travel, following, with a new hope, the well-worn traditional routes of their world. They carried each his own present from his own place; and these things were the things they dealt in and the roads were the roads their people habitually followed; and nothing but the star and the purpose were new.

Christmas, from the South Arabian landscape, was no longer the gift that comes unsought, joyful and unexpected; one was far away from Bethlehem, which was as it were the receiving end. Here one set out on the life's journey with nothing but the dark hard landscape like a vast barrier before one and a star whose light shines on a horizon out of sight. When our Arabs in their slim white gowns, with swift movements and small hands and light feet, had brought us our Christmas dinner, I went out and looked for a long time at the volcanic edges of the land against the night and at the foreign constellations of the south; and wondered where among their galaxies that one had appeared which surely should be called the Traveller's Star? How difficult, how vital to choose it; how safe, how eternally hopeful to follow it; and to find at the end no great attainment of splendour, but something intimate and fragile and secluded, willing to accept the gifts we long to give.

1953

Round Perim in Wartime

A convoy moves in gay and gentle sunlight along the Red Sea way. It carries merchandise and oil. Along the narrow floor of waters low tankers, their funnels set back like Arab boys on donkeys' cruppers, creep two by two, each shabby stern a bare few hundred yards from the bow of the tanker that follows. Sixty thousand tons of oil are here, ready to go up at the first torpedo.

Because of the dangers of a route sunk as a lane in hedges in the trough between Africa and Asia, no convoy hitherto has threaded the Red Sea. Not, that is to say, since Italy entered the war. Therefore there is a certain elation in watching the White Ensign flutter so arrogant from the mast of our cruiser in the sun. We ourselves are dangerous; our cargo is ammunition. We are protecting the flank – 'left back' as it were, our destroyer being goalkeeper behind us. Restless as a sheep-dog, she zig-zags from side to side and flickers yellow sentences in morse from her high shining towers. She is black as a thin-backed fish as she cuts the sea towards us; then pale and almost invisible as she turns and trails a pathway green and smooth behind the teeth of foam that bite her sides.

The sea is all intersected by these pathways cut by the racing de-stroyers and by the fleet altogether as it turns to zig-zag east or west. An aeroplane circles in the sky, its three engines round like birds' breasts in the sun. From the cruiser in front another aeroplane is catapulted, and springs, light as a butterfly, from its iron home. We are a well-girded caravan. There is a gallant air about us – those small and rusty oil ships, the deep round-bellied merchant-men, the wolf-like grey destroyers – all banded in fellow-ship together. Slowly and leisurely we move (for the tankers go slow); our men, clad in a minimum of shorts and tennis shoes, are strewn in patches of shade about the decks; through the hot Red Sea hours the crews lie sleeping, ready – like someone in a legend or a ballad – to spring at a word to life. The guns are manned both fore and aft, their surfaces caressingly and ceaselessly polished with small brushes by devoted crews: eight look-outs are on the watch for periscopes among the ridges and dancing crests of waves; an alertness is hidden behind our curtain of repose. And now as the twilight nears and we reach the straits of Perim (bombed earlier today), our warships line up in a broad avenue to see the tankers through. They stand one behind the other in the mirror-light of evening, in which the yellow lighthouse shaft revolving begins to gather strength under a daffodil sky; the tankers push on side by side; far off, in sunset, Italian hills are there in sight, silent and inoffensive; they leave little doubt as to who is master of the sea.

Our galaxy floats on like a family of ducks across a pond, small, but with an empire behind it. With many centuries of history behind it also, I think as I watch it and see in its grey forms the ghostly outline of many a small armada, different but similar, of such as have handed down from age to age their simple heritage of valour. Norse seamen on Massachusetts beaches before they had a name; Channel fleets of the medieval traders carrying – in spite of French in ambush – their Flemish-woven cargoes of wool; the Cape of Good Hope, the Straits of Magellan, and raiding parties in the Spanish Main; privateers under towers of sail a hundred and forty years ago; we were good raiders before being masters of oceans – we would not have let Spaniards charged with gold pass by our doorstep as the Italians let us slip by charged with oil.

Watching this power that moves gently as a dream into the quiet shades of evening, it comes upon one to wonder why this power should be. What gives it birth and what will keep it? It has been with us so long that surely it must be ingrained in the stuff of which we are made.

It comes, I think privately but not frivolously, because we do these things *for fun*. For a generation perhaps, or more probably for half a generation, you can stir nations to heroic lusts by theories and sounding names; permanence goes only to those who enjoy what they do. And there is no doubt that these sailors enjoy themselves. In our particular ship they have mostly not been bred to the navy: they are R.N.V.R., drawn from offices, factories, suburbs – until six months ago, scarce one had travelled a hundred miles from London. They are 'keen as mustard', their captain says. The signal lad is from an insurance office: he stands now barefoot, with brown young shoulders, flashing back answers to our cruiser. The two gun-teams vie with each other in polishing and timing their guns: they came into action for the first time some weeks ago and the aft gun has a grievance, for the captain did not swing out to give to both a field. She does not hate Germans, or Italians either, but hopes that soon a better chance may come. As for the forward gun, she accomplished fifteen rounds a minute, but hopes to make twenty another time; one does not want war, but it is natural to enjoy things when they come. Against such pleasures simple and profound the doctrines that irritate our century are bound to fail: for the joy of being a Fascist or a Nazi palls with time, but the pure pleasure of hitting a bull's eye is, humanly speaking, eternal.

Aden

In clean moonlight Aden Grater shows like a broken bowl of ragged earthenware, its rim cracked into points against the sky. A great circle, high in the south, tilts these jagged edges down to where the town lies flat and dark, close to that point which the volcano's lava, breaking through, once pierced to reach the sea. These ancient wars were followed by a peace now ancient in its turn; washed by soft air, those gaunt precipitous ridges seem ever to have stood just so, in an immobility splashed only by the alternate lights of night and day. The town, too, has taken on this timeless immobility. Its brown houses are indistinguishable in the night; its lights are shuttered; its inhabitants sit quietly at home; only rarely do motorcars with pin-prick lamps obedient to the black-out show like small specks of its primeval fire in the volcano's lap.

Through this dark peace, built on the silences of time and sealed by the fears of man, three muffled wails come riding through the night – air-raid sirens from Steamer Point and the European harbour, dulled by the rocky mass between; their curious banshee voice is followed by dull thuds, the deadened fall of bombs.

As the sound is five miles away, we do not take cover but sit on the roof and watch with fascinated eyes the terror and beauty of war.

Eight searchlights are out. They leap into the sky behind our rocky bowl which seems to gaze, absorbed and dark as a theatre, towards the illuminated stage. Pale, phosphorescent green, the long giraffe-necks hesitate and hover and, like spokes of a fan, concentrate high in the sky; the moon is just above. At the meeting-place of the searchlights, within the green light and the outer, milder radiance of the moon, shaped like a cross and held in an evil halo, is the Italian raider. He is, they say, about 6,000 feet up. And now the sky about him breaks as it were into spangles, small jagged golden flashes that mark the bursting shells. Smoke is invisible in the night; only those shattered lightning fragments of gold tell that the sky is tremulous with death. From behind our volcano wall the noise beats up like surf on a beach, constant and angry; the ships are in action too. Four or five at a time in hurrying streamers, red fire-balls like incandescent soap bubbles rush up from behind our wall into the sky and die. And over all this turmoil, strangely reassuring, the moon continues to ride in her smooth light; the rocks whose heart has cooled so long ago keep their impassive and majestic outline; the town lies deathly still below. The raider flees, caught in the pincers of the searchlights till he escapes to the outer darknesses that hangs above the ocean; the wounded are gathered and the dead; and the friendly bells come ringing through the streets to say that all is over.

It is a fashion now never to speak of the beauty of war. When the B.B.C. gives us the description of a raid, it takes pains to see that Mr or Mrs Snooks tell us about it in language strictly appropriate to the commonplace. It is probably our moral sense which (rightly) disapproves of war and (wrongly) assumes that it is therefore ugly. Not so the Ancients who behind the tragedy of Ilium could see the features of Helen. 'The face that launched a thousand ships' is more difficult to recognize when you call it by a name like Democracy; but it is ever a fact that Beauty is made not less but more beautiful by the neighbourhood of death. The fragility and transitory grace of things inspire their human loveliness, and it is the measure in which we feel it that gives us the measure of delight. War, that brings so much of horror, yet gives this poignancy of beauty. It arises no doubt from the greater sensitiveness created in ourselves. And I am confident that many a young man in the future will forget the shrieking towns and burning houses long before the memory dies within him of some stray morning hour, when, with the sleeping world enchantingly about him and the sky just waking, he sets out on an adventure that may bring no return.

1940

Arab Background

A short time before the last war it began to be surmised by those who are interested in these matters that the Suez Canal could be dispensed with. The greater power of the far sea-going ships, the farther flights of aircraft, were able to make the African bend with no fatal dislocation of the trade of east and west. It was for some time an academic question, yet the future of the British Commonwealth was known to depend upon the answer. And when the war came, and the matter was put to proof, the allied eventual victory was for a time dependent upon the answer too. From June 10, 1940, when Italy entered the war, until 1942, when Allied superiority slowly reopened the Mediterranean, the Suez Canal was eliminated from the vital factors of the situation.

What Mussolini did by his gesture and the consequent closing of the rea-route was to put the seal upon a process which began with Vasco da Gama and the discovery of the Cape of Good Hope in 1497. The opening of the Suez Canal was not one of the decisive events in history; it facilitated a main route which was in use already, and – however great the difference between the old East India Company's land journeys and transhipments and the comfort and directness of the Canal – it cannot be compared to the importance of the Portuguese discovery, which diverted the very pattern of civilization and made the Mediterranean become in fact, if not yet in the eyes of men, 'the tideless dolorous Midland sea', the sea of an immensely beautiful decay; the main stream of Asian trade took to the Atlantic. A student of history can see this at a glance by watching the precipitous decline of cities; Rome and

Byzantium, Cairo of the Fatimites, the wonder of its age; Antioch and
the other great trading cities of Syria; Venice, Genoa, Marseilles, and
Barcelona: for century upon century the world's riches passed through
one or other of these sea-gates of Europe; their revenues provided
the markets, their navies and their caravans the means. With Vasco
da Gama's return out of the West, and the Atlantic rise of Portugal,
Holland, France, and England, the decline is swift and obvious, and so
general that only a general cause can explain it. The discovery of the New
World added its magnetic attraction to the West. The Mediterranean
had become a backwater: though the Suez Canal reopened a sluice,
though Marseilles and Alexandria recovered and a partial ripple of the
main stream once more poured through, the Atlantic road had become
the main road in fact, and Mussolini's fatal action merely emphasized
what had long been obvious, and showed the Mare Nostrum – let the
adjective apply to whom it will – to be no essential thoroughfare to
anything beyond itself.

The genius and comparative stability of Italy and Western Europe
disguised this process under the splendid trappings of art. But in the
Levant, the countries of Arabia, lying along the bridge of Europe and
Asia, afford a clear index of the fluctuating importance of the trade
route. Most travellers today through these remoter parts still find their
best guidance in the writers of the ancient world or in those Arab
geographers who carried the new religion along the roads of the old
merchandise between the ninth and fifteenth centuries of our era. A
map of Arabia as full and as accurate as that of Ptolemy could never have
been produced again until the nineteenth century revived the world's
curiosity, and the love of exploration for its own sake made people like
Burton attempt to 'remove that opprobrium to modern adventure, the
huge white blot which still marks the Eastern and Central regions of
Arabia'.

In the darkness between these two periods what is most remarkable
is not the obscurity of Arabia. Trade routes are both delicate and
tough. They depend on supplies and security; if these are interrupted
their life itself is suspended; and yet they find their way like water.
Palmyra, destroyed in a week by Aurelian's conquest, watched the long

camel-trains make for the same eventual goals through the stone-cut bazaars of Aleppo. City after city rises and sinks on the great trading routes of the world, but while there is demand at one end and supply at the other, the route, like a chain of ants, will wriggle to one side or another, but will exist. In the case of the Arabian countries, the decline of Roman wealth and the barbarian invasions annihilated for a time the *demand* for Asiatic wealth. Hence the decline. The Dark Ages buried even the knowledge of Arabia together with the books in which it was preserved. (Strabo was only translated into Latin in the fifteenth century.) But as the Mediterranean and European world settled into relative stability, the demand for the Asiatic luxuries revived; and the supply found its way not only through the immense difficulties of the overland trail, where the Roman or any other peace no longer obtained, but through the iron curtain of the Crusades as well. The history of Italian republics in the Levant bears witness to the triumph of trade over politics and even over religion. Iron, timber, slaves, the essential sinews of war for the Saracen forces, were continuously provided by the Italians against their allies, while pepper and spices needed for the salted winter meats of Europe, and the luxuries bought in the growing courts, poured through in a constantly increasing stream.

The medieval civilizations of the Levant, Cairo, and Byzantium, flourished in the lap of the trading routes from India and China; together with their silks and peppers they took the transmitted learning of the ancient world to the north Mediterranean shores. The library of Monte Cassino and its medical renown, the popular verse of Sicily, the chivalry of Provence, the Spanish romances, all bear witness to the influence of Arabia. Christian rulers like Frederick II encouraged Arab learning and introduced the arts and industries of the east. A few years ago, when the tomb of Cangrande della Scala, Dante's host in Verona, was opened, he was found wrapped in a silken shroud round whose edge words of the Qur'an were woven, the product no doubt of some Sicilian loom. The scope of the Arabian influence in letters is perhaps the most remarkable of all. Even as far north as England an astonishing number of Arabic books were translated in the twelfth and thirteenth centuries: the first book ever printed there, in 1477, came from an

Egyptian-Arabic original. Adelard of Bath, early in the twelfth century, travelled in Syria and Spain, translated Euclid and other works from Arabic into Latin, and returned to be a tutor to Henry II of England. Benjamin of Tudela gives a lively picture of how the Jews could wander from synagogue to synagogue across the hostile frontiers at this time; and on the eastern side of the curtain are the Christian populations, the Armenians, Maronites, Chaldeans, etc., sellers of provisions to the Mecca caravans, who made things easier than they would otherwise have been for the Crusaders. Behind the pageant of war and the banners of the crescent and the cross, it must never be forgotten that the Arabs continued to be the only middlemen of the trade with Asia; the most valued goods of the Middle Ages, every bundle of pepper, every bale of frankincense for the cathedrals of Europe, came through their hands. Owing to its very difficulties and dangers, the ramifications of this trade spread into every cranny of the Arabian world. It was diverted by Persian wars, by Carmathian raids, by Turkish invasions. In the course of centuries, stretching far back in an age before Islam, this trade permeated the lives and consciousness not only of the merchants in their cities, but of the poorest, wildest camel-man along the endless tracks of the caravans; and this mercantile background, comparable to that of England or of the United States but much longer in duration and influence than either of these, should ever be remembered in any assessment of the Arab of today. He is essentially a civilized man and a trader, and the background of two millennia and more is not to be destroyed by the decline of a few hundred years.

If the Asian trade had continued to flow through the Mediterranean, it is I think safe to say that the Arab world would have recovered both from the Mongol and the Ottoman invasions. But the Cape of Good Hope was rounded only forty-four years after the fall of Constantinople; and the Mediterranean decline took on the speed of a catastrophe all over the Levant. The advent of the Turks and their destructions have distorted the picture; they are blamed not only for the ruin they actually brought, but for the absence of recovery which followed it. The fundamental geographical reason for this absence of recovery was the opening of the Atlantic, and this is illustrated by the fact that European interest in the

Arab world now shifts to the south. The Indian Ocean, the sea-route of the spice trade from the Cape, and the lands that lie about it, begin to re-emerge from the centuries of their obscurity; before the end of the fifteenth century a Spaniard, Pedro da Covilham, is first in South Arabia, touching three times at Aden on his way to India; John Jourdain, on a trading venture, is sent officially to visit the Imam of the Yemen in his capital in 1609; Portuguese, Dutch, French and British – all the Atlantic powers – vie with each other and negotiate to snatch the inheritance of the long Arabian monopoly of the Indian trade; and in 1839 Aden is bought, conquered, and occupied by the British as a coaling point on the long haulage to India, at a time when the invention of steam had made it essential for a sea-going power to refuel at fairly close intervals.

This development of the Atlantic thoroughfare barely touched the Arabian lands of the south and its chief effect on the Arabian character perhaps lies in the suppression of piracy which attended it. The incidental cleaning up of the Persian Gulf and its coasts by the British navy laid the foundation of those local treaties and friendly relations which eventually made possible the agreements for and the exploitation of oil. And this brings us to the key of modern Arabia.

In the normal course, the Mediterranean decline, ever more strongly marked as one travels towards the east and away from the Atlantic sea-lands, should have continued uninterrupted until the closing of the Mediterranean made it visible to all. The coming of the aeroplane, like the opening of the Suez Canal, would have brought a flicker, but only a flicker, of revival; the trade route of the Levant was essential at first, but, as the range of the great cruising machines grew longer, the African routes became as easy as the trans-Arabian, and the endemic tumults of Arabia would not have been worth negotiating in the interests of air transport alone. Oil came into the picture like one of those geologic intrusions by which a whole landscape is changed. By its discovery the countries of Arabia have once again become what they were for two thousand years of their history, the middlemen for one of the world's most valuable products, with the addition that the product is actually located, for the most part, within their territory. Until oil is superseded in the world, the lands of Arabia are bound to be immensely important.

This historical preamble is, I think, necessary to any assessment of the Arab character and its prospects in the modern world. The acquired ingredient has been fostered over so long a stretch of time that it has become as much a part of the human creature as physical characteristics due to other causes. It is, I imagine, only the repetition of causes over a great time that *does* create the differences between human families. However this may be, I should say, in assessing the modern Arab in a general way, that four main influences must be borne in mind. The first is a natural liveliness of mind, a very remote characteristic whose racial origins we cannot trace, but which is visible right through history in the ease with which new things are attempted. I would take the Arab's adoption of the sea as an example: this not only carried him across to Egypt and to the doorstep of Byzantium within less than a century of the death of Muhammad, but it still sends whole villages of young desert-bred men to travel, as stokers and such, on the trade routes of the world. An old bedouin sheikh who had never seen a sheet of water was taken by some friends of mine to a picnic on the shores of a lake in Transjordan. They all went to swim and he joined them; and when he was asked how he managed to keep afloat, since he had never before seen a mass of water, he answered: 'Of course one can swim. All animals do so by nature.' And he did. This quality of initiative will be recognized by all who have had to introduce modern gadgets in the Arab lands.

A second influence on the Arab character is the *desert*. The desert plays the part which the Alps or the sea-coasts play in relation to the prosperous and easy-living urbanized districts of other lands. It feeds them with a constant trickle of healthy, hardy, and resourceful human stock. The first history of civilization is largely the history of desert immigration into the fertile crescent. The process is continued all the time, in a small and unobtrusive way; so that while one may discount the actual *desert-living* Arab as an influence in the modern world, one must yet remember him in the same way as one remembers a feeding stream by which the waters of a pond are kept alive and full.

The third ingredient is the historic influence of commerce mentioned above, and continued over so long a period of time and over so widespread an area both of desert and city land that it has fully entered into the makeup of practically all the nations of the peninsula. It is this ingredient, I think, which produces the remarkable political intelligence and grasp of remote, international affairs, which every traveller notices even among the most primitive societies in Arabia. They talk about the affairs of Europe or the characteristics of America as they once talked about the gossip of Samarkand or Cairo; then as now, these regions so far removed had a direct bearing on Arab lives, and made themselves felt along the nerves of the trade routes – once round the camel-saddles in the Khan or caravanserai, and now round the wireless.

The fourth ingredient that is moulding the Arab of today is the development of oil. This influence is of course only recent; its effects are likely to show some points of similarity with the ancient development of Arabian riches, but new factors in transport and the increased likelihood and facility of outside interference make of it to all intents a new opening of Arabian history. It will bring riches, and it is already doing so, on a scale far greater than that of the ancient trade. What is even more revolutionary, it looks as if it may bring fertility to a very large desert area as well. A subterranean water-level runs below the desolate eastern coast of Arabia under a rock-cap that only the powerful deep-boring modern oil-drills can pierce: as they make their way, and the surface desert is reached by water, the geography of all this great area can change; the eastern shore of the Persian Gulf can combine a sea approach (though poor) with the richest oil wells in the world within easy stages of it, together with a territory that in a short while can be made to blossom like the rose. The fact that most of this oil will continue to be carried by pipelines overland to Levantine harbours for shipment towards its markets in Europe, means that the benefits are bound to be divided among a good number of the Arab nations. Saudi Arabia, Kuwait, Iraq, Syria, Transjordan, and Palestine are all in for a share of production or transmission if the geography of markets continues to be what it is now. With such a fountain of gold in their midst, it is certain that there will be an increase and not a decrease in the schools and hospitals, the mechanical luxuries, and the ease of travel which year by year are Westernizing the Arab populations.

The most interesting point about the Middle East oil development is that it is being carried out by the West European and American companies on non-competitive lines. An illuminating article in the *Middle East Journal* for January 1948 describes this process and the necessities underlying it:

> 'Not only is new entry to Eastern Hemisphere markets hard and costly; any significant shift of relative market positions is equally difficult. If any one of the seven large oil companies attempted to augment appreciably its share of the available market, it would not only have no assurance of a successful outcome from the effort but it would needlessly and fruitlessly break the established price and profit structure, to its own detriment as well as to the disadvantage of competitors. Such efforts have occasionally, but very rarely, been made in the past; and the attempts have always been regretted. The international oil trade is an almost perfect case-study in oligopolistic competition; and it is against all the logic of oligopoly for one firm to act in a manner which it knows the others would not, indeed could not, tolerate.'

America came into the Bahrein oil as a result of a mistake made by British experts in their assessment of the evidence; they underestimated the treasure and let it slip. I remember a good deal of disappointment at the time, and I also remember thinking even then, in 1933 or soon after, that the advantages to Britain of an American entry into the oilfields of the Middle East would very soon far out-value any loss of actual oil wells. The inevitable result is already becoming apparent; regardless of any temporary divergences – the Palestine question is a case in point – the eventual interests and policies of the two powers are showing themselves to be identical. The result of this on Arab development is all in favour of stability: the game of playing off one against the other – tragically dear to weak nations and small – is becoming obviously less advantageous year by year, as the overwhelming excellencies of united action become more widely realized. If the world's future lies in the hands of the Anglo-Saxon powers, this picture of stability, with a steady Arabian development towards a Westernized prosperity, might be confidently predicted to continue. As it is, the Russian factor is particularly present on the oil-world border; the choice of two roads is continually pressed on every thinking Arab of today, with the disquieting knowledge that his immensely important, barren lands may at any moment be the centre of a conflict on which his whole future will depend. He is faced with the old clash which often paralysed the spice road, when the empires of history fought for the markets of Islam. British and American action in Palestine in past and present has encouraged this threat to Arab stability and has also produced a cohesion of resistance throughout the Arab world. It is, however, to be counted – one must hope – among temporary and not permanent influences. What is permanent on the other hand, and largely a result of the oil development and its attendant prosperity, is the rapidly growing importance of the middle class.

This can be watched in various stages in every nation of Arabia. The mechanism of modern life needs technical experts; these have to be produced through education; the education creates the middle and professional classes. When these grow strong enough, internal tension arises; a reaction against older forms of government and the people who supported them. Much present xenophobia is due to this purely internal cause, since foreigners have naturally dealt chiefly with the established leaders who were governing Arabia, and it has long been obvious to careful observers that there was a danger of unpopularity in being too exclusively identified with the patterns of the past. Both in the yet primitive and faintly stirring societies of central and south Arabia, and in the almost Westernized cities of Egypt, the process is fundamentally the same, since the whole future of these regions is bound up with the development of oil, which in turn makes a Western system of society inescapable – bureaucratic, democratic, totalitarian as the case may be, but inevitably bound up with the rule of the professional, technical man.

Iraq, a conveniently halfway house in this development, may be taken as a typical example of what is happening in the Arab world today. I cannot do better than quote from a very able summing up of the recent crisis there which appeared in the *Arab News Bulletin* of March 12, 1948:

'The crisis proved decisively that the Iraqi intelligentsia has become a very powerful factor in Iraqi politics. This class of educated young Iraqis is organized in three parties: The Istiqlal (Independence party), the Ahrar (Liberal party), and the Democratic party. All three are Nationalist parties with social programmes . . . you find almost every educated Iraqi a supporter of the parties, and you find many who are active members in one or another of them. Indeed all three parties have so far shown a remarkable degree of co-ordination and have taken a uniform stand on all major problems.

'Ten years ago these parties did not exist. The only forces in Iraqi political life were the old politicians, the landlords and tribal sheikhs, and the army officers. . . . The new parties of the intelligentsia have strength only in the cities. The number of their active members is very small and their strength in elections is also very small. But they command a powerful press, and they form intelligent public opinion. Their potential strength is far greater than can be deduced from their actual numbers. Besides, with their better organization, their social consciousness and their proclaimed programmes of reform, they are growing in number and power daily. The old generation cannot ignore the new rising intelligentsia, partly because of its growing political influence, and partly because it is indispensable for any sound administration.'

This might now be written of any Arabian nation in the north – Iraq, Syria, Transjordan, Palestine, Egypt – it will not be very long before much the same will be true of the south and centre also. For the forces of geography are the strongest forces, and on them the history of nations ultimately depends. It is due to them, to the difference in fertility between the Fertile Crescent and the deserts which feed it, that the Westernizing of the Arabian patterns marches with such diverse steps. There is an interesting point in connection with this in the recent history of mandates. The mandate was designed to safeguard the principle that states not yet fully civilized (at the end of the first World War we still believed in civilization) are to be helped and not exploited by the nations deputed to look after them. The interesting point is that in Arabia the mandates were applied not to the *more* but to the *less* primitive regions. The justification is simple. The primitive societies, under very fine individual rulers, were well able to manage a simple sort of administration, whereas the more advanced north Arabian nations were trying out a civilization on Western lines, in which they needed guidance and help. For the same reason, it is difficult at the moment to predict personalities in the future of the north Arabian lands; the Westernizing pattern of democracy deals with communities and parties, and to point to individuals at this moment in north Arabia would be to tie oneself almost certainly to the past. The young effendi has not yet won his right to a name among the many pioneering statesmen, able and courageous, who have brought their Arab world out on to the platform of history; and it is to be hoped that this comparative obscurity may continue, in peaceful semi-anonymity of democratic ways. But if the storm breaks again, and pours – as it most certainly would – towards the oil-fields, the Arab background, its native wit and courage, its desert history, its long experience of world-wide dealings, will again produce some great and individual leaders, as it has done so often in the past.

1949

When these essays were being collected, with old papers appearing from forgotten hiding-places, the following three stories met me to my surprise. The first of them I had lost so completely that even the year and place of its writing are uncertain, though a Baghdad garden in the summer of 1943 seems the most likely; even so, with its dim recollection floating through my mind, it seems hard to realize how and when I found the time to write it out. The other two tales go back to my girlhood in Italy and the first World War. There they had lain, with yellowing edges in an old portfolio, and there they were going to be once more decently entombed if a friend, who kindly looked over and helped me to select these essays, had not urged me to include them.

I have done this, though their dates and order do not strictly belong to a book of essays; but their background is the same, and shows a last flicker of the long shadows of war that conditioned the life of my time.

Musical Interlude

Where, in the twilight gulfs of the mind, do the borders of sanity end? Is there a line, a single step to be taken, as it were a watershed to cross – or are there angles and dimensions unknown which make the discoverer free of so strange a universe that he becomes incomprehensible, like a world behind a mirror, and therefore insane to his fellow-men? The subject came up lazily, on a summer's afternoon, with light on the lawn and a scent of hay coming in at the window; and John, just demobilized, told me the following story:

'You know', he said, 'that I was stationed with a lot of people in the depths of the country and what a god-forsaken place it was – the small amount of things to do there were not nearly enough to go round the numbers of us at the time? It was one of those lulls that come in the middle of a war – all routine, work for work's sake, and we were all hoping for the weeks to pass and bring us back into action. The M.O. told me he had never had so many nervous breakdowns to deal with before. "All the musical chaps seem to be going bats", he told me.

'Music was one of the few distractions obtainable. There was an exquisite pianist. I won't tell you her name, and you might not know it, for it is years since she played in public. She lived in a big country house with a garden full of trees, not far from the camp, and she used to invite batches of men and officers to play to them. Now and then some favoured young man would be asked alone to spend an evening listening to her. She was an elderly woman, rather sallow and with a shapeless figure, dressed without any care in black; her face was interesting – one of those faces that have been so much made by their later life that you have no idea what they looked like when they were young. It is always rather depressing when you see exactly what a young girl looked like in a woman of fifty, isn't it? Anyway, she was just herself, and one couldn't imagine her either younger or older, or even any different if she were dead: she had a kind of immobility. Her black eyes, with very black eyebrows, looked as if they were registering, but any reaction to the registration went on far behind that carved exterior, out of sight. This made any sort of emotion or initiative of hers surprising; and I had this feeling of surprise when, having been taken to her house one evening with a large party, she asked me as I left to come again and listen to some Brahms by myself.

'I went, and it was incredibly pleasant. We dined, and then she sat at the piano and played. The room was gently lighted, and the notes seemed to fall like flower-petals from her hands, moving white and agile, and alive as it seemed with a life of their own. It was a warm evening of late summer and the glass doors were open to the lawn.

'"Would you like to listen from the garden?" she said, without moving or stopping in her playing. "It sounds better in the open."

'I thought this a good idea and stepped out. The night spread veils of silver like spider webs over everything beneath the moon. The trees were sleeping on their shadows in the grass. The colours of all the flowers except the white had faded, but the garden was filled with scents and a freshness of dew. It was like stepping into peace, and the music from the lighted room poured out and wound its way among the little paths and beds of flowers.

'I can't remember how I noticed it first, or by what steps the change came. The first thing I realized clearly was that the notes of the music were moving towards me. I can't explain. They were not visible, but I *knew* that they were tangible. They were still at a distance, but they were taking up positions for attack: they were grouped in the shadows of the trees, avoiding the patches of moonlight. A sudden cold discomfort made me move towards the door, and I noticed that I was intercepted. The notes came pouring out; singly, in arpeggios, strung along the paths between the roses, or gathered in groups of chords where the pathways met: as they reached the garden from the lighted room, they instantly became silent, malignant, and alive. I moved, and they moved, keeping a circle around me – not near but, I *knew*, growing nearer as their numbers increased. I can remember quite clearly two stages of horror – first the knowledge of their separate existence, and secondly the moment of realizing that they were hunting me. It is impossible to make it clear to you, for I never saw anything. They were essences. They were there, and I was aware of them; they were increasing and increasing between me and the lighted drawing-room. Their world was abnormal but quite real. By remaining in it, I suppose I should have proved myself mad, and yet I know I was no different from what I am at this moment. As it happened, I was saved, I don't know how. A turquoise amulet I collected in Palestine and always carry for luck was in my pocket: I felt it as I thrust my hands in, clenched in a sort of frenzy. I don't suppose it was the amulet – it was probably the association: but I made up my mind I could push my way through that unsubstantial army and I did – up the rose path; as I went, they moved slightly, but nothing touched me: I stepped across the low sill into the drawing-room where the sonata was ending. My hostess rose from the piano: "You have come in quite soon," she said.

'I have never been able to decide whether she knew or not. You can imagine that I was glad to leave. I made a point of seeing the M.O., and found that the "musical chaps" he spoke of were all among her listeners. We were scattered and I was moved to France, and have never met any of them since. But where the border-line lies between my sanity and their madness, who can tell?'

1943

The Dead Comrade

Late in the summer of 1916, in the very height of the Isonzo battle, Lorenzo dell'Adda was sent to Venice for a draft of new men, and incidentally for three days' rest after a sleepless fortnight on the Carso.

His fresh, rather cherubic expression had become almost haggard under the long strain. When he reached Cormons, suburban and peaceful in spite of the military occupation, he turned aside among garden walls to the hospital to ask after his school-friend and C.O., Captain Rainieri, wounded some days before. The Captain had died early that morning.

Dell'Adda was too exhausted to feel acutely, but a great weariness came over him. The gravel path he stood on, with a smell of disinfectants hanging about it from open windows; the wistaria in heavy bunches over the gateway, dark gaps against a dark blue sky – became blurred in his excited vision with endless lines of yellow trenches – two hundred miles he calculated exactly – clutching the whole of Italy from Adamello to the sea. His friend's voice in the centre of it all came unnaturally clear, joking over some government blunder, as he had last heard it.

And then it all passed.

The light was brilliant round him – not barren and stifling as on the Carso, but shimmering on the horizon and restful in sombre patches of foliage. There was leisurely traffic on his way – camps everywhere, and mules patient in the dust, flicking slow tails, their heads in a scrap of shade; in the distance, some peasants cutting maize; and the car sped with a delightful humming song over the smooth straight road.

In Udine the young Lieutenant had a wash, a shave and haircut, and at last felt ready for Venice and his holiday. 'It is not quite Milan', he reflected, thinking of other occasions: 'but there must be a few women left; and I shall stay at the Danieli, and forget all this . . . We shall see . . . ' And he stumbled across the darkness of Udine station to his train.

There were two women in the carriage he entered – silhouettes and no more in the general blackness. They sat on opposite sides, both dressed in black. One, a broad rather shapeless mass, he took to be no longer young. The other, a slim shadow, sat upright in her corner, the ray of a dimmed lantern outside catching a finely-shaped hand with long fingers on her lap; her features were quite invisible, and dell'Adda could only distinguish a colourless oval. He took his seat beside her on principle, and waited while the train filled, suddenly aware of being really tired.

The passengers came slowly, stumbling and muttering to themselves over the darkness of the way. They were practically all military. Three officers climbed in and settled down with the usual formalities of introduction. Then a civilian, 'probably the only one on the train,' dell'Adda thought. It suddenly made him realize that it was unusual to travel in female company through the war zone, and he began to wonder what the women were. The one at his side seemed scarcely to breathe, she sat so still. He shifted very gently so as to be nearer, till his left hand came up against some prickly woollen stuff – a cloak no doubt. Without a word of warning the train began to move. It jolted out among ghostly trucks and engines, out into the night of stars; the telegraph-posts began to pass like sentinels in swift succession; the travellers seemed to have settled down to sleep.

'What are three days,' said Lorenzo to himself. 'I shall be back in that Hell in no time. One must live at double speed to get even with fate nowadays.' And a thought of the dead Rainieri came unbidden, like a quick spasm.

He looked at his neighbour. The train was jerking roughly from side to side; his shoulder seemed to be resting against her coat.

Was she asleep? Her head was bent very low, quite lost in the darkest shadow. He ventured his hand a little farther, and touched a silk dress, very soft and agreeable. And she did not seem to mind! He allowed his hand to rest there against the warmth of her body, while a delightful languid feeling of well-being crept over his weariness: he was not thinking of the war now – not thinking of anything at all – he was falling asleep; he was too tired for adventures really.

In his half-conscious state he felt vaguely that something was happening. Was she holding his hand? One needn't go far after all he reflected with instant lucidity and ingratitude. But this was rather extraordinary. She was raising his arm, pressing it close to her breast; she seemed to be stooping towards him. With a great effort he tried to draw himself out of his drowsiness. He could feel her heart beating against his forearm through the thin blouse: it crossed his mind that he would have preferred to postpone all this for a day.

Then some scent came like an intoxication and wrapped him round: she was moving; he turned also; in the darkness their lips met and held each other. He gave one swift thought to the trenches: was he not paying off the long months behind him? And she held him with a sort of passion, as if she would drink his soul.

She must be quite young. His face rested against her neck, soft and warm, he was in her arms like a child. She would not let him go – would not let him move even: when he stirred she bent and kissed him, on the mouth, on the hair, on the eyes, and held him faster with a sort of desperate strength.

The train swayed with an even rhythm, running quickly now across the starlit plain. Its rumble fell into a steady tune; it seemed to be carrying a load of shadows among the shadows of the fields outside. Dell'Adda abandoned himself to the motion – to a will that was stronger than his own – to his excessive weariness. He slept without a dream.

*   *   *   *   *

When he awoke the dawn had not yet come. The earliest light was flowing grey and cold.

At first all was vague in his mind. Then he realized that he was still in the stranger's arms, his head on her shoulder. He was amused: she must have held him without moving all the night.

He put out his free hand and gently stroked the arm that supported him; but there seemed to be no response. With a slow and careful movement he screwed his head round, so as to see her face.

He was pleased. She was indeed quite young – dark hair, pale, a gentle mouth with very sweet lips – surely not what he had expected! She looked simple and quiet. Her eyes were turned towards the window. And then, seeing the face as he did at an angle from below, he noticed that she was weeping silently, apparently in an agony of sorrow.

The Lieutenant's surprise was such that he remained petrified for a few seconds. Then he began to feel extremely ridiculous. He raised himself gently to a more independent position, the young woman making no objection. As he rose she looked up with a faint blush as if on the point of speaking; but her eyes did not reach his; they seemed to be spellbound by the regimental badge on his collar; she tried to speak but could not, and bowing her head quickly under the black hat-brim appeared to be absorbed in a paroxysm of grief too overpowering for words.

The sleepers now began to stir. The train was making for the fringe of the lagoons. Dell'Adda felt that the flavour of his romance had departed. There seemed to be no escaping from the realities and sorrows of life. The young woman's emotion was real enough; he thought of her passion in the night and could not help feeling that that also had been genuine. Only why? And for whom? Not for him, surely! His vanity suffered; he felt injured. There were rules in the game and they had not been observed. Was she going to sit there without giving him even a look? He stood out in the corridor and watched while the bowed hat-brim remained provokingly motionless.

Dawn was approaching in level yellow bands, and white houses showed, and all the details of vineland and corn. Venice was very near. There was a bustle down the train as the police came to verify passports. Dell'Adda listened and gathered that both the women were going south: he would have to leave them at Mestre and there was an end of it. A feeling of real anger took hold of him: why should he be troubled with tears and problems during his short three days? And what was it all about anyway?

He pulled down his bag; they were running into the station, and he was already opening the door when she came out, looking painfully embarrassed: 'You must have thought it very strange,' she began, stammering. 'I feel I must say something . . . I have been to see . . . my husband . . . You will not understand . . . He died . . . an hour before I came . . . at Cormons. . . .'

She paused as if to get breath. The people were pushing by, and she became more agitated and incoherent. 'You belong to his regiment I see . . . of course you cannot understand . . . I think I have been mad with sorrow. . . .'

'Your husband? My regiment?' cried dell'Adda, forgetting his chagrin in a quick presentiment. 'Will you tell me his name?'

She seemed to shrink away, hesitating. Already the doors were being slammed up the train. Then, looking up, their eyes met and she must have read what he was thinking. 'Captain Rainieri,' she said, scarcely above a whisper.

1919

An Eclogue of War

Joseph's father owned a large homestead and a number of oxen in the province of Turin, where the river Po lies between poplar banks, like a mirror to the Alps.

In May and early June the cattle-owners, who winter in the plains of western Piedmont, and the shepherds of Provence, who live on the flat lands of the lower Rhône, gather their flocks and herds and make, by walking stages, for the highest grazing lands of the Maritime and Cottian Alps. Here the people of the two rivers meet, and hither Joseph and his father would also come with their cattle.

Any town or village at the foot of these hills knows the yearly procession, tramping leisurely in a cloud of its own making, whose fine dust coats sheep and sheepdogs and the dinted velvet of the shepherd in the rear. Somewhere in the crowd, jingling with bells and harness, are the mules who carry a gipsy-looking medley of all that may be necessary for the summer home. The women perch on the high wooden saddle or 'bast'; the small boys learn their trade in the dust with the sheepdogs and settle into the long stride, the swing of the pole, and the silent ways of their elders. The herd may number several hundred and plods along with a heavy padding noise that never pauses. You may hear it go by on summer nights with a clanking of bronze bells – bells of Camargue, with huge bodies and narrow necks where the clapper hangs like the tongue out of a dog's mouth; and the harsh sound comes with the remembered freshness of the hills to all accustomed ears.

Across the plains, already heavy with summer, the mountain shapes draw nearer. Their phantom outlines darken and take on the contours of reality – till the first chestnut glades rise gently, opening long grateful avenues of shadow. The hills gather round; the slope of the road increases as it keeps by the torrent, crossing and recrossing, its view ever cut off at sudden corners by the steep profile of the valley. Small streams tumble with delicious voices as of laughter, and the grass grows so deep that it seems to live in a twilight of its own beneath the sun. The air is sweet: weariness is lifted away like a pack: and the men, who have wintered in farms amid country business, gradually fall back into their mountain stride. Their eyes are filled with quietness, and the rocks and the silence and the clear light subdue them.

All the winter through Joseph would think of these things, and on still evenings as he drove the slow cattle homewards across the gathering haze of the plain, he would look up to the clear flame-shaped point of Monte Viso and its long snow ridges, whose unearthly horizon became without his knowing it a symbol, an overshadowing necessary presence in his life.

When the summer came he went with his people, up the valleys beyond the farthest village where the mule-track ends, beyond the last trees, to the birthplace of torrents and the discoloured places of the snow. They always took the same grazing land, rented from the parish of Bellino, with pointed rocks all round it in a hollow bare to the sun, and a brook ran over stones in shallows through the middle.

From above, as one toiled up the col, this place looked like a bowl with broken edges, or some volcano crater mapped on the face of the moon, with the grass in a thin carpet and patches of rock showing through. One could stand upon the col and see how the Alps run east and west in long parallel lines with the clouds and deep gullies between them, away into the distances of light; and the height was such that one seemed to feel the roundness of the earth and watch her very motion in the infinite serenity of space. The hollow, with its pointed rocks, looked absurdly small, like a coracle tossed about in great waves; it was only after a long descent that one noticed how it was in truth an extensive plain, with grassy hills and valleys of its own and numerous small water-courses that ran down every crevice into the central stream.

Joseph had spent every summer there since childhood. When the war came, and he was enrolled among the youngest recruits and sent eastward to billets near the frontier, he would get away as soon as he could after the evening rations, roll himself up in his short cape, and while the star-shells danced on the ridges and the searchlights pointed their hesitating fingers over the crouching land, while rattling supply columns passed in the darkness and all was preparation for tomorrow's battle, he would go back in memory over every detail of the mountain road. As he fell asleep the noise of the lorries came to him as the voice of rocky streams.

He was kept for a summer and winter on the Carso or near it, sometimes right up among the trenches, sometimes in rest camps between the maize fields beside the straight roads. It was a new and difficult world, and the pictures in his memory gradually lost their keenness until he came to pass several days at a time without consciously recalling them, aware of them only through a vague discomfort that always lay somewhere beyond the reach of his thoughts.

Then in May 1916 there came a time of bad rumours when the Austrians attacked down the valleys that seem to grasp from Trent to Lombardy like a hand. Every day the officers looked more anxious; and every day more batteries, and stores, and ambulances were sent westward rapidly, till Joseph's battalion in its turn was loaded up on lorries and rushed across Venetia to the foothills of the Alps.

The battalion unloaded itself by the roadside and rested for an hour or two; then filled its water-flasks at the stream, shouldered haversacks, and marched off, a long swinging line of steel helmets.

Joseph remained. He was told off with some others to guard ammunition in the shelter of a dell – a quiet place, shut in by grassy shoulders from the sights and sounds of battle. The road curved round the hill and the stream fell below it in a series of small pools hollowed out under the turf, and the noise of the guns travelled round and round it among the echoing mountains as if trying vainly to find a way in.

To Joseph it was all like a dream. He scarcely heard the guns. He was back again among the things he knew, and the scenes of the past year were suddenly as unbelievable as if they had never been. This was not war: he stood on mountain turf and the gentians were opening at his feet.

As he kept watch through one evening after the other, and the valley filled with shadows and the dampness of the dew, and the whole sky shone remote and pale beyond the slope, it seemed to him that the sides of the hills receded into lines he loved and remembered, and he saw his *grangìa* on its mound of black earth where the cattle had trampled, and the outer wall enclosing it with loose stones, the fire built up by the door where the soup was cooking and the sheepdog lay across the threshold watching his coming with lazy eyes and slow wagging tail.

The grass was in flower: a deep fragrance came to him with every breath of wind. Soon, he thought, they would be cutting hay; in the transparent shadow of the twilight, anemones showed like a milky way across the darkening meadow.

He thought of Marie, whose father came from Provence with a flock of sheep and shared the pasture land, who spoke the patois of the south softer than his own. He had known her every summer since he could remember, hunting barefoot for marmots among the boulders, or stretched out in the shadow of the rocks as they watched their flocks through the hot hours. He could hear the whistle of the marmot now if he shut his eyes: it was sudden like an alarum, and they used to creep to where the stones began and the grass ended and all the outlines were blurred in the heat – and would see the little creature sitting up on a boulder, bending its small furry body this way and that as it shouted out the signal of danger.

He used to help Marie when she carried water from the stream. She was strong, squarely built, and seemed when she stood still to belong to the earth as permanently as the rocks. Her arm was quite round and hard and smooth, with dimples at the elbow, and she had a fair skin under the sunburn – quite fair, and light eyes, like the edge of the sky when you see it against the hills. Her flaxen hair was drawn tightly in a knot as the peasants use, with a few little curls that blew about her face: he had seen that colour often in the maize fields of Friuli when the sun had bleached them the long summer through.

The remembrance of his dusty year of war filled him with unspeakable longing.

Night had now fallen: the stars came out: the hills were soft as velvet. The road lay below like a dim scarf and a line of lorries was crawling along it carrying the unending load of shells. Above the noise of their engines the little gurgling stream seemed to glide in a silence of its own as it fell from pool to pool.

If anyone had told Joseph at this moment that not many miles away his companions were being killed he would not have believed it. Yet the Austrians had reached their last obstacle before the Lombard plain; they could look down from the heights of Pasubio and see Venice in the distance; and in a struggle for the mountain's lower slopes, her regiments melted away.

Joseph would have fought had he been there. He was no coward and had never known real fear, and would hazard himself without a thought for a straying lamb or to guide a stranger through the snow; if Italy in his mind had been one with his fields and familiar places he would readily have given his life and asked for no reward.

But to him, Italy was a name talked of in the newspapers. He saw no connection between the Austrian advance and his distant hills. He was alone, his work as it seemed a mere formality invented by the government; he saw no use in standing day after day a solitary sentinel in that lonely quiet place. He never reasoned the matter out: but the pictures of his own highlands and the scent of the coming hay filled his mind with images that crowded like a witchery in the night of the hills. When the first ambulances came down from the front in the darkness, he waited by the roadside and hoisted himself up unobserved.

He travelled four days and nights, hanging on to steps of railway carriages, hidden in trucks under the tarpaulin – always making for the west. When he reached his first depot, the point of his battalion's departure, he left the railway line and started walking across country. In all this time he never allowed himself to give one thought to the reasons or consequences of what he did.

Late in the afternoon of the seventh day he reached the *grangìa*. His father stood with a scythe in the long yellowing grass: the mother was down by the stream washing some crimson garment that caught his eye far away. They asked about the war. 'It will not end yet,' said Joseph. 'It goes on just the same, always.' He would stay a week or so for the haymaking, he thought, and then go back and explain to the *tenente*. He felt the vague disquiet which he had so persistently refused to formulate in his own mind, and steeped himself in the joy of his home-coming to suppress it.

He fetched the scythe and set to work with his father in the meadow and cut the hay till sunset. Then he went down to see Marie in the lower *grangìa*, and was asked many questions and praised for his great cleverness in escaping, and told them all about the war and the rich lands of Venetia. As he went home through the fading light his soul was filled with peace; he thought of Marie, how strong she was, and hard-working, and an only child; of the number of her father's sheep, and of all the future before him.

The days went by and still he meant to return. Meanwhile there was much work to do. In the evening when they had milked the cows they made cheeses, one every day, and piled them on shelves in the dark interior of the grange till the autumn when they would sell them all together. They saw only such rare travellers as crossed the col and gave them news: the Austrians were driven back, the war was going on just the same as ever. Once a week the father went down to the village with the mule and brought back a load of meal and bread and faggots and told them what the schoolmaster, who read the papers, said about the Germans.

Then, one morning, as Joseph stood outside the *grangìa* sharpening an axe before beginning the day's work, he saw two military policemen in the grey-green uniform making their way down from the col across the boulders, and the incubus that had been lying at the back of his thoughts so long unrecognized came before him clearly. These men had come for him. He realized that he was a deserter and all it meant.

He stood there, sharpening his axe like a machine, till they came up and showed him a paper: they were Italians from the south – he could hardly understand them when they spoke. They were taking him with them. His father, standing in the doorway, looked on with a puzzled expression, not following the quick speech and only vaguely realizing that it meant absence again, and Joseph's return to the war.

The words came quickly: for Joseph also they had little meaning at that time. His mind filled, as when he came, with the picture of the life he was leaving. He felt a dull pain which he remembered long afterwards, and he walked slowly between his two guides. When they reached the top of the col, where one may get a last view of the hollow and see the *grangìa* and the stream and the lower *grangìa* farther away – small like toys with the cattle browsing round them – the vision of it all came before his eyes in every detail, clearer than he had ever seen it. He did not need to look.

1919

The waves went over, the shadow became manageable again, the delightful variety of life was back, lifting its head timidly here and there under economic pressure. Mexico and Greece were new or renewed for wandering and marked, as far as I was concerned, two novelties that made their deep impression: a visit to Mexico and the bull-fight – the world's cruelty moulded into beauty, a vision infinitely majestic after the cruelty of war – and the deciphering of the Greek-Minoan script which was then being made public; this opening door of history bewitched me and, unknown to myself, was gradually drawing me away from the Arab East towards the Anatolian bridge of Greece and Asia.

The Bull-fight

The whole of Puebla seemed to be on the way to the bull-ring that
winter afternoon. The 23,000 people for whom there was room
on the benches were certainly there. The owner of the Royalty Hotel,
a plump and comfortable man, looked surprised when we asked if he
was going. 'I never miss,' said he. 'I killed twelve bulls myself, as an
amateur, when young.'

We had read our Hemingway; we had been in Mexico City and
seen the new matador, Rafael Rodriguez – '*recien-doctorado*' as a paper
with wide views on education had called him, or '*el ciclon hydro-calido*'
(because he comes from Agua Caliente) according to the posters. He was
appearing in Puebla with Velasquez and Procuna, the most accomplished
of the Mexican matadors. I longed to hear again the trumpets that sound
from high up on the tiers of the arena, so that the Spanish fall of notes
drops, strange and remote, from the sky. We were also anxious to
see if the bull was frightened. So we asked for places near the barrier,
'close to the capes', in the shade – and this sign of intelligent interest
brought the best tickets and a number of pats and handshakes from the
host of the Feniz Restaurant, who was evidently a patron, for we saw
him embraced in the friendly Puebla way, held breast to breast with a
series of small jerks and strokings from behind, by one of the victorious
matadors.

The church and the bull-ring must surely have been the two great
instruments of success for Spain in Mexico. Aztecs were used to long
processions up the steps of the pyramid, to the sacrifice pinned down,
the ritual of death; the bull-fight must have come as a new presentation of

something very old and deeply settled in their blood. The stiff dresses of the matadors heavy with gold, of the picadors, of the peons, are hieratic garments. They are evolved, as are the vestments of priesthoods, by the rolling over of long usage and tradition in time. Every movement, every action of the ceremony has been so evolved – up to the supreme moment when the matador, standing with joined feet, sights the bull's head along his outstretched arm and sword, and reaches in above the charging horn to drive home.

When the president of the arena has taken his seat and the trumpets sound, and the alguazils have backed out their horses, and the matadors, walking slowly with their helpers behind them, have saluted their public from the sanded floor; when the fighter of the first bull has changed his brocaded cape of ceremony for the magenta silk that means business, and the sand has been brushed over and the red-barricaded space is clear – then the closed doors of the toril open (very briskly from the outside) and the creature whose death is certain dances in, gay, confident, unaware. A classic sense of tragedy is given by his unawareness and by the beauty of the young animal – the great neck where his strength lies, the slim flanks and small light hooves, the thin tasselled tail that floats as he charges, his blackness against the silken toils of cape or muleta; and his belief that the world is his to play with, that the game is all his own.

The peons trail their capes, the picador is down and the bull pushes into the stuffed panoply of the horse in vain, the banderillero with his two barbs held high stands solitary in the centre of the arena and stamps his silk-stockinged feet and calls the bull to charge him; and now the torero comes with his red cloth in his left hand and weaves his adversary about him in dangerous charges foiled with silk, until – with a half-turn, a *paso de recorte* – he plants him with forefeet so turned that it will take him a few moments to recover. He walks to take from the barrier the thin sword with curved tip that is to enter the small vulnerable place. At every moment of this ritual, and most especially as the matador bends over with the sword, a flicker, a sigh of wind for instance, may lift the red cloth and the bull's head after it, to pierce the neck of the swordsman with the point of the charging horn – at any moment the bull has it in his power to turn from the silks that flutter about him and rip his enemy. The Spaniard ennobled the sacrificial ritual by placing the life of the priest in danger, and this is the real novelty brought to the ceremonies of the Aztec pyramid by the Conquerors.

To those who cannot avoid looking on the movement and colour with eyes attuned to ballet, there is always a third actor on the floor of the arena, the unseen dancer, death. The audience see him, and shout their hoarse, short, unanimous shout of '*Olé*' or '*Toro*' as, tricked by matador or bull, the invisible presence grazes by between the swinging cape and the embroidered breast. The bull alone is not aware of him, misled by the strength that is in him, by his inexperience (for he has never had dealings with men on foot before), and by the flicker of the empty silken garments, the vanities of his world. It is tragedy, where everyone may see himself, the plaything of the gods and danger. Perhaps this inspires in the audience a care for justice for the bull within the limits of the rules. When a picador placed his spear too far back a shower of angry cushions flew down from the seats above, though he was unhorsed and on the ground and the bull nuzzling, to his obvious discomfort, at his feet. The object of all that happens until the matador takes up his sword is to weaken the tossing muscle of the bull's neck, by which a horse can be lifted and which no man can cope with in its full strength; and anything beyond this, a pique too far back that may injure the ribs, a banderilla wrongly placed, is greeted with disdain by the packed rows of the amphitheatre. In the short span of fifteen minutes allotted before death, the victim and the matador must play their parts, and any dereliction offends those who distribute applause or blame.

A strange thing happened. One out of the six bulls of the afternoon was no fighter; he had one horn shortened and splintered and poor sight: and Luis Procuna, the most elegant of the matadors, played with him in contempt and finally let the time go by, till the doors of the toril opened and four steers appeared to lead him away. He went, herded among them. Twice he stopped, reluctant, and snuffed the barrier, where the man with the cape was standing behind his little shelter; but the steers drew him in their aimless herd, and he drifted out to a poor death outside and we felt a sad pity unknown for any of the fighting bulls who, when they felt the coming strangeness of death, laid their heads on their folded knees as if for sleep. The day was over. Rodriguez El Ciclon, eighteen years old, stood in the arena with every handkerchief in the audience fluttering above him, while someone cut off the ear and tail-tip of the last bull, awarded by popular applause. Then the youths of Puebla in an adoring crowd lifted him on their shoulders and carried him through the streets to his hotel.

1949

Royal Tombs at Mycenae

The traveller from Corinth southward, when he dips over a low pass and leaves on his right the road into Arcadia, or he who comes north from Argos, or the islander landing at Nauplia and crossing lowlands grown out of the sea: all these, if they turn their eyes to the northeast, may distinguish against heaps of mountain bleached like bones the darker mound of Mycenae. It looks low as you approach it, though firmly wedged on a saddle of the limestone between abrupt ravines. But as the road rises, the Argolid plain begins to stretch away; and ranges behind ranges appear like petals of roses, delicate pencilled outlines of farther hills. Below the lion gate of the Atridae, by the Perseia fountain house whose stones Professor Alan Wace has this year uncovered, whose waters – long deviated – now nourish the modern Mycenae village below, one may look from end to end over the outstretched lands of Argos and see their loveliness, dangerous as the eyes of Helen, and saturated, too, with murder.

A climate of doom clings to the citadel and its fragments of polygonal walls and empty beehive tombs; there is nothing here of the tranquillity of Olympia or health of Epidauros; the night comes down with a stillness louder than noise, a silence of things that have happened and exhausted themselves long ago. And now, out of the past of this Past, legends four centuries older than the Trojan War and the fates of Agamemnon, new forms emerge – an earlier dynasty of kings and queens, nameless but substantial in their bones.

Dr I. Papademetriou for the Greek Archaeological Society has uncovered the most dramatic find here since the days of Schliemann. A

cemetery, a stone's throw west of the Perseia fountain, has already
yielded six unrifled graves, and promises more from the excavations
continued across and below the roadway where tourists without knowing it have been treading the earth that shrouds the oldest northern
invaders yet discovered in Mycenae. They lie as they died, stiffened as
death found them, in whatever attitude of anguish or repose; some on
their right side, in a quietness of sleep, with knees gathered and the
cheek pillowed on the hands; two, in the largest tomb, lie stretched at
length, and between them, with strong knees firmly separated, a chief
whose end found him seated, perhaps on his throne. His height is near
six feet (they are all huge for this Mediterranean world); his teeth are
intact, even and bright; a fierce and almost gay vitality seems to inhabit
those bones so resolutely laid. Round the heads of these three, fifteen
bronze swords and knives lie scattered, with loosened hafts of alabaster
and ivory that remain; the Wood has perished. A cauldron and large
vat of bronze are there in a corner, with pottery – brown or cream in
opaque patterns, or glazed orange or cream – fashions of the Cyclades
and Melos copied by Helladic craftsmen. There was a wooden casket
(perished); a masque of gold, two golden cups and a most delicate cup
of fragile earth with a laurel branch in relief sculptured on the handle.
At the men's feet, belonging to the same tall northern race, a woman
lies with clasped hands, her lost and ageless pain still locked in her
closed fingers. It is moving to look down on the various postures, mo-
mentary gestures whose duration was to be nothing, which the rigour
of death has captured for three thousand and five hundred years. The
dating of these discoveries is pushing the whole of Mycenae backward
into time, and the inhabitants of the burial ground, still held in the wall
that was originally built to enclose them, belong to an age before the
Atridae, perhaps to the first descendents of Perseus, somewhere about
the seventeenth century B.C.

They were buried in shaft graves (although as I write a chamber tomb
has also been discovered). The largest grave was lined with unbaked
tiles, and covered with wooden planks and then with rushes; and over
these a layer of waterproof clay which has kept the print of the more
perishable things below. Above them two stone stelae have been found,

carved in relief with bull and lion hunts, and with the fine wave-pattern of the Mediterranean (already familiar to the neolithic carvers of Malta). Over the smaller tombs, a covering of slabs suggests by their number that they may have been shaped into a gable roof, like a house. The funeral feast was held by the open grave, and earth shovelled later; and the tombs were reopened and bodies pushed to the edges to make room for new inmates as they came. These things the archaeologists infer from animal bones found in the graves, and from the skeletons disarranged after their death: but of what went before, of their names and their story, no history is apparent, except what is written in the tall northern structure of the bones and skulls, for anthropologists to measure later on.

The most articulate discoveries have been made in a private house of the thirteenth century B.C., excavated for the British School of Archaeology in Athens by Professor Wace. Here a number of inscribed clay tablets burnt (and probably preserved) by the burning of the house, have an importance whose full value can only be realized when the key to the language is found. The unlocking is very near: the numerals are known already, and it is almost certain that the language will prove to be an early form of Greek written in the Minoan script.[1] These tablets are the first ever to be found in a private house; they are accounts, columns of words followed by figures, and show how much more diffused than we were disposed to think it was the thirteenth-century art of writing. On the back of one of these tablets, as it might be on a blotting-pad in a modern committee room, some Mycenaean scratched a glancing figure with slanting eyes, a careless trifle full of grace – probably the first doodle transmitted in history.

Perhaps one of the chief interests of archaeology to us, the unscientific looker-on, is the salad which it makes of ancient and modern. Among his finds, Professor Wace has a little dump of tools, chisels, a double axe, a hammer beaten in bronze but ready for use by any workman today – the perfect, simple shapes have not changed. But an ivory only two centuries older belongs unmistakenly to its own art and day: it is the curved section of a tusk, twenty inches in length, with a griffin and the feet of an opposing griffin broken off against it; in its small compass the whole speed and vigour of that Mediterranean world are gathered; the sure and delicate lines have a long tradition, foreign to us, behind them; and the tusk, Professor Wace told me, was taken from the elephants of Syria, long since extinct.

1950

After a war, there naturally comes a resettlement of values, as well as the general, material rebuilding of life; one looks back over a dyke and is surprised to see how much has been left behind on the farther side. Happy those whose luggage was of that sterling quality that continues to be useful on the later stretch. During the late forties spent at my home in Asolo and busy with essays written for *Perseus in the Wind,* the abstract pattern seemed more and more clearly to underlie the compass of my days, and the four following papers all deal with abstract themes; and I thought then, and think now, that this opening of our human landscape, so closely woven with all the terrestrial things that have made us and yet so free, is the joy and the emancipation of age.

The Old-fashioned Spinster

I met again the other day, for the first time in years, or so it seemed to me, the spinster of my childhood. She lives in a cottage in the hills, alone, surrounded by cows, dogs, poultry, and the lively business and management of a farm near by. She has the pale blue eyes, the slightly faded outline – as of the third or fourth and not the first impression of a fresco – which I so well remember; faded, one may speculate, by some stress in the past, but now definitely and patiently reconciled: and she is a centre of small activities – children, relations, public affairs, the poor. Yet there is a feeling of stillness or arrested time about her: perhaps because she is no longer thinking or caring much about the passage of time.

How have they all disappeared, the innumerable elderly women in small households, inhabited usually two by two, in country or suburban cottages with gardens? Most often they had looked after some active and dominating parent, who died leaving them middle-aged and poor. And then they made the best of it, and found a school-friend, or some grey-haired vestal similarly dedicated and derelict, and settled into a life that flowed through much the same landscape as before but with a little stream of liveliness and independence unknown under the filial strain.

To the free women of today whom one would not dare to call spinsters these lives must appear as unendurable stagnation: and yet I remember an atmosphere of contentment, a spaciousness almost, in their dealings. This came no doubt from the absence of any need for planning, the quiet expectation of tomorrow extremely like today.

They mostly travelled. The maps of Europe were criss-crossed by their itineraries, frugally dotted with *pensions* where an easel or a sketch-book might flourish on the picturesque. This spinster's network was superimposed, almost without touching it, on to the political, economic, restless, unimaginable world in which even the most casual traveller takes an interest today. It was not luxurious. It catered for school teachers and poor daughters of country gentlemen, admirals, curates; and it was a perpetual surprise to see how many of them there were and in what unexpected places.

The First World War began to shuffle them out of sight, and the following slump precipitated them into a limbo where the second World War destroyed them. The spinster as I remember her in my childhood is practically extinct. The world thinks little of her loss and her modern successor now looks back on her with pity as to a creature in chains. Whether she was much more in chains than anybody else, is one of those questions that requires more investigation than we have time for: but it is intriguing to know what made her happy and preserved her moral stability in a world in which we now see Freud at every tea-table. I have often looked for the reason, and have come to a conclusion such as it is: I believe that much of a spinster's happiness was due to the fact that her chastity was an asset in her day.

Let us, for instance, imagine what would happen if our highest praise were offered to cooks: if the excellent among them were invited to the Guildhall every year to be crowned with sage and parsley and entertained as public benefactors: without any increase of salary, with only the breath of honour, the cook would reappear serene and contented in our now mutilated homes.

It is hard to find anyone so poor, so miserable, that he does not partly live by the breath of honour: often without knowing it, and often seeking it blindly by dishonourable paths. Surely no error was so gross as that which invented purely economic man?

We have taken the spinster's peculiar honour away. Nobody now expects her to be chaste, or troubles at all about this aspect of her life; if she is so, it seems a silly thing to be. Chastity is a negative virtue, and has perhaps had an unduly long innings in our immediate past. In the days of its power, it rode roughshod and harsh over more permanent humanities: it showed little mercy and is reaping none today. Like many virtues, and indeed more than most, it took to the letter and mislaid the spirit of its teaching: I am not out to see it reinstated in its former pomp. Nevertheless it made spinsterdom an honourable estate. The elderly woman with sensible shoes whose clothes no one noticed was not a failure: she had not been merely absent-minded in her youth, an Atalanta stooping for toys; and she was able to feel herself in the straight for her goal.

Perhaps, when she saw the Atalantas of this world darting here and there, a thought of wistfulness might come. (What a lot of trouble, incidentally, seems to be connected with the apple in mythology; no other fruit is so potentially destructive.) But, whatever her private feelings, the spinster's public credit was safe. The unmarried woman today must have a career, recognition – a barbarous word – and all sorts of help to make her status bearable; there is a feeling of restlessness, an instability about it all; even academic honours, one feels at the end of life, may not be enough. This subtle insecurity is due to the fact that the heart of her world is against her; no one sees any particular virtue in women unmarried just for fun. The old-fashioned spinster was embattled on the citadel of her community: the virtue she practised was intelligible, simple, and attainable by all: with the disappearance of chastity, the climate she lived in departed, and the spinster of my childhood is no more.

1949

Tidiness

Tidiness, in spite of the concerted effort of humanity to teach it to the young, is one of those virtues that never will be assimilated with pleasure. It makes life easier and more agreeable, does harm to no one and actually saves time and trouble to the person who practises it: there must be an ominous flaw to explain why millions of generations continue to reject it. Possibly it is some rule of nature which makes things go together, like pink eyes with white fur in rabbits, and the Siamese twin of tidiness may be so disagreeable as to inspire a revolt against both. I think myself that instinct, more reasonable than our teachers imagine, inspires our distrust; it is a form of fear; we realize that tidiness is not a thing to be taken for granted, like a minor but indispensable piece of domestic furniture: it is one of the forces of nature – basic like salt in food, to be treated as an essential but to be used with discretion. To have a force of nature pushed at us without explanation from the age of three or thereabout, and ever after, by all persons in authority from our nannies onwards, is bound to be disconcerting.

The greatest of mythologies divided its gods into creators, preservers and destroyers. Tidiness obviously belongs to the second category, which mitigates the terrific impact of the other two. Even the darning of stockings, when looked at in this light, acquires majesty and becomes a victory in Time: it is as if the Vestal Virgins found a half-way position for their thumbs and the fate of a material object is not averted, but delayed. The trouble is that there are now so many material objects in this world. Who does not know that secret joy, when turning out an old store-cupboard, of finding something so decrepit and tattered that, without any moral hesitation, one feels justified in throwing it away? I think it is Walter Hickey who describes the dinner parties in the India of his day when the cheap Canton ware that we would now give so much to own was taken up with the tablecloth and shaken out of the window. I once spent some weeks in a hospital with working women and found that not one of them ever darned their underclothes – they were cheap and it was easier and less expensive to buy new. Every modern invention that increases the multitude of *things* brings creation and destruction closer together: the only way to counteract this terrifying tendency is to make objects ever more beautiful and elaborate, slower to finish and more delicate to possess, and such that their value in our sight is sufficient to make tidiness a pleasure.

This once occurred in my childhood with the gold and silver tinfoil in which chocolates were wrapped. After their first pleasant brightness, these scraps were thrown away, until someone told our governess that, if made into a sufficiently heavy ball and sent to some missionary society, they might eventually redeem an African slave; the tinfoil acquired a halo of romance; it was smoothed and flattened out and religiously (that is the word) plastered on to the growing weight of its predecessors and it made the eating of chocolate meritorious, a sort of ritual of liberation, pleasant to all concerned.

The fact remains, however, that tidiness is not a theologic virtue; every religion I know neglects, if it does not despise her; she has fallen among the small bric-à-brac cherished by officers, governesses, employers of labour; she has indeed become utility rather than virtue – a mere device for the preventing of trouble from other people.

I am convinced that this is due entirely to her own arrogance in wishing to set up for herself alone. Apart from the sunrise of creation behind her and the night of destruction ahead, tidiness has no separate existence, she is merely a conveyance, a mode, a transition, a putter-to-bed of ephemeral things, a handmaid in short. Yet like many handmaids today, she is out for independence and goes about expressing herself in a regardless way, an enemy instead of an ally in her trinity, cluttering up creation and delaying destruction with no care for either. If anyone is in doubt about this, let him go to places where tidiness is loved for herself, sheltered in files and clichés and mummified in forms and let him take the nearest form – of which there is now no lack – and reading it, see how the meaning evaporates in its desire for order: instead of the variable garment fitted to each occasion as it comes, the pigeon-hole is invented, monotonously square and so generally accepted that it threatens our civilization and perhaps our life.

I have been an official myself and kept an office and have no quarrel with files. When I started, I decided to have forty of them, partly because this seemed a reasonable number for our needs and partly because it is a lucky number in the East. When we reached it and a new document appeared demanding private space, someone went through our forty and weeded out the weakest, distributing its few essential papers among the most suitable of its neighbours. I still think this an excellent way of keeping files, as it made us look through them at intervals to see what they contained and it must have had a salutary effect on the papers themselves, saving them from that most prevalent of diseases in Government offices, the feeling of their own importance: at any moment they were liable to destruction, just as we all are.

This surely is the way to look upon tidiness – not as a mere machine for hoarding, but as an arbitrator, with the whole world of created things on one side and annihilation on the other. What dignity is suddenly conferred on this rather drab little Cinderella among the virtues, if she will forget herself and think only of the two great claimants who demand her perpetual choice!

The archaeologist is perhaps the human being who gets the most comprehensive view of tidiness through the ages; the trifles she has selected to keep, the maddening gaps in history due merely to the loss of what she threw, away! Thousands of heavy little clay tablets engraved with accounts, forty centuries old or more, encumber the museums of Asia and Europe, while things we might have enjoyed, the love-letters of Semiramis for instance, have long since found their way into whatever it was the Assyrians used as a waste-cylinder basket in their time. And this has been done partly, of course, through wars, rapine and invasion, but very largely through ordinary people like you and me, clearing out their cupboards and their desks.

Tidiness in her most charming aspect is the handmaid of creation, devoted and sincere. But for her, what would remain of our endeavours, the thoughts we have written or painted, the things we have made? The sum of our achievements goes on, like those Triumphs the Renaissance was fond of painting, crowding all its variety on the slow car of the ages, scattering the road of its passage with treasures and toys. And the little maid, you or I or anyone, follows after, humbly pedestrian, keeping this, discarding that, deciding what is to live and what must perish; when we look upon what she has preserved for us out of the welter of time, or think upon what in careless moments she has dropped in among the rubbish – the words of prophets, the dreams of artists, the glories of craft – we look with admiration and also fear at this unassuming little virtue, the first; with which we are bullied in the nursery.

1949

Greed

One is puzzled to think why taste, and greed its follower – comparatively innocuous among the five senses – should have been singled out into a deadly sin. Pride, anger, avarice, envy, sloth and lust: greed seems a minor squeak in the catalogue.

Lust, you may say, deals with the senses. But in a distributed, generic way. Shakespeare places it in its niche as a waste of *spirit*. It is not, like greed, one sense in excess, but something quite different and more abstract, which makes a wrong use of our material tools that attend like courtiers or panders to help it to its ends. It uses them all, some more and some less, according to its particular bias; for there is a difference in degree, but no radical difference, between looking, talking, hearing, touching; and the man who enjoys pornographic pictures is not really more innocent than he who goes to bed. Perhaps the contempt of the normal woman for the philanderer is just this – that he is lustful on the cheap. Lust, therefore, though a deadly sin, is evenly distributed: all the senses (even, I am convinced, the listening to bad music, or poor cinema) are implicated; while greed is singled out for solitary opprobrium.

Not religion, but the arrogant, arid, theological mind creates dislike for a physical body which the gentleness of Christianity begs us over and over again to look upon as the temple of God. It is strange to the modern reader to notice how often Shakespeare refers to this image as axiomatic, a truth understood and accepted in his day. In the decent robustness of our creed the union of human bodies in love symbolizes that of Christ and His Church; the whole of our tradition confirms the innate nobility of all common tools of life; and the parable of the talents might easily apply to our five senses, given us to spend in service with all our power, under pain of displeasure if we leave them wilfully inactive. If we come to think of it, every sacrament deals with the most material, the most brutally physical things that can happen to us – birth, marriage, death and digestion. After the messiness of the womb, the baptism of life is given in common water; our degradation into earth is the moment chosen to transfigure us with life eternal; and the holiest sacrament, based again on the simplest, cheapest, most basic as well as most cheerful food of man, is inextricably combined with the procession of our daily food. Are we to think this unintentional, or not rather hold it for an affirmation of the grandeur of life itself for creatures on earth?

The incidental union of lust with the senses has produced an almost inconceivable amount of unhappiness and misconception. Over it, people appear to lose their reasoning power. No one would believe that Bach or Beethoven are not to be played because human fingers are unworthy instruments with which to interpret their music: yet a whole army of Puritans in various disguises have decreed that one part of our anatomy is more or less taboo to the divine. No mother would agree to think one bit of her child's body different from another; no nurse would think so in a hospital. Fingers are objectionable if they draw ugly pictures or play ugly tunes, and the organs of sex should be used only for the transmission of love. Our senses are not the mainstream of life but merely the banks through which it flows, clear or muddy as the case may be: to keep them clean and smooth and pointed in the right direction is all that we have to do with them – and to see that, if possible, more than a trickle of the river of life finds its way through them – for the sources of *that* are very far away. Only saints or waifs will risk a short cut, trying to jump ahead of earthly instruments to find themselves in what – in a provisional way – we may call heaven or hell. For only a very, very few is it safe to risk this leap into the void, unprotected by the kind and comfortable guides which life has built up for us out of the first protoplasm in time.

All our acts have sacramental possibilities – like Greek masks made out of the current pasteboard of commerce, through which the drama of the ages spoke. Perhaps even the unconscious violation of sacraments produces our sense of sin. I have thought of this in the case of elderly people pointed out to me as homosexuals or lesbians: emptiness draws over their faces with the coming of age and this has puzzled me for a long time, for in the Muslim East, where such things are very common, no similarly damaging effect appears to follow. I have come to the conclusion that because this intercourse is outside our tradition and forbidden it has lost the sacramental character indispensable to love (which is, for instance, plainly visible in the Platonic dialogues) and therefore a desolation has come over it, as it does over a loveless marriage or any other profound human relationship whence, from one cause or another, the sacramental character has been removed.

The thoughts of our days write themselves on our faces and produce, with the coming of age, like the tiny, imperceptible hammer strokes on beaten gold, the hardened surfaces with which our life must end. Not the act, but the flame which kindles it, burning behind and within the activity of our life, creates this substance. The acts count in their inward effect and if love is their solvent can save even beyond the boundaries of law. If this were not true, what could we make of the words of Christ to the adulteress? Even murder, no doubt, may be pure and the angels of pity stand at the bedside of Desdemona. Yet the fact remains that neither murder nor adultery are spiritually safe, and if we are contemplating either and are poorly satisfied with the laws and traditions that have cradled us, we can still find our answer in the underlying sacraments of daily living. If I had a child growing up in the normal questionings and rebellions of youth, this is the advice that I would give; never either to break or to keep in with convention except in harmony with that feeling for the sacredness of life of which the sacraments of everyday things – salt and oil and water, earth and bread and wine – are the deep and lasting symbols.

And why, with all this, is greed a deadly sin? How cautiously the Seven have been studied – not (as by modern philanthropy) for their danger to society but purely with an eye to their mischief in the individual soul. Anger, greed, envy, avarice, sloth, lust – and pride, the worship of Self, the sin of Lucifer. Poor little greed, for which any way we have so little scope nowadays and which does nobody except oneself any harm, why is it in this company? Perhaps there is a negative reason. Taste alone among the five senses in unconvertible to love.

Let us think of ourselves as Shakespeare saw us, sanctuaries of divinity even when produced by —

Their saucy sweetness that do coin heaven's image
In stamps that are forbid;. . .

In this pleasant light, the grace of love stands by to illuminate touch, hearing, sight and even smell: not one of these but can and should give or receive a pleasure that in its transient moments bears the stamp of eternity. But there is no occasion that I can think of when eating — not even the spick and span lobster or the first asparagus of the season — helps with love, except of course in the utilitarian way, that actual hunger must be removed. Taste is the only one of the five fingers that cannot be used for playing Beethoven or Bach; the excess of it is therefore incapable of good. So it was popped in among the Seven, to my regret. But perhaps just because it is the humblest among the senses, excluded from the sweet ante-room of Paradise, tied to the earth and symbolical of the worm — perhaps because of this bankruptcy it has been lifted into honour and the greatest sacrament takes, in kindly compensation, the dark and lowly road by which our bodies and souls are united on this earth.

1951

This I Believe

In a rather easy but none the less heartfelt way I hold to my church's teaching, and among its points of faith will select, for this short summary, the trust in immortality as that which has the most influence on my business of living as a whole. It must indeed make an enormous difference to the architecture of one's life – to have it cooped inside a century or to be freed into eternity. I feel this most practically as I grow older, and am enabled to look peacefully on my age as a beginning and not an end, so that the sense of adventure which has always made me happy can still continue with me. The vagueness of the ideas I hold on immortality does not trouble me in the least – for it would be a poor secret that could lie within the grasp of a human understanding. My godfather, when asked what he felt about a future life, said that he trusted 'to the ultimate decency of things' – and I am content to leave the details to this great 'decency', with a complete faith that we have something wider than Time to move into through our gates of being. It seems to me that everything temporal, from our human relations, our smallest daily activities, to the policies of nations, must be subtly altered if the scale we work to is that of this life only or of eternity – and for better or for worse, I believe in the larger scale.

Within this framework I believe in Curiosity – a disinterested delight in the truth of things for their own sake, entailing a dislike for anything in the nature of slogans, advertisements or clichés, any twisting of words away from their sincerity, any mass-production in thought, anything in fact which throws another obstacle on the already so heavily encumbered paths of truth.

For I believe that, under its many facets, the enduring Unity inside the world is half hidden or half seen according to one's seeking; so that, if we have enough sincerity, every smallest act of our days can be a sort of union with what is everlasting. This is the sacramental view of life which the Church illustrates, building its symbols with everyday necessities like bread and wine, salt and oil, water and dust – the things man has used and needed from his earliest times: and this continuous sacrament that binds us at every moment of our time to something that is beyond time and yet within us – this constant existence in eternity is what I most deeply believe in.

Only in this climate underlying time can we get away from the loneliness of life and really meet our fellows. The self-walls, in their innumerable variety, shut us in – and I believe that it is only in the union or communion beyond self that any human relation – of marriage, of parenthood, of class, ideology or nation – can eventually stand.

1953

These three essays all deal with the art of recalling or *communicating* journeys. Subsidiaries to the art of travel, they build, as it were, a bridge between the nomad's life and the writer's desk and are a part of the slow and pleasantly *double* experience of a vagrant life.

The Travelling Reader

I have been asked to write on travel books and why I read them – a subject on which my own readers are more qualified to give an answer than I am. I travel too much to take more than a few such works about with me, and though I know fairly intimately why they are written, I should be more put to it to tell why they are read. The reflection, however, that I am too deeply involved in the actual business of travel to read about it very often, makes me conclude that a sedentary life is one of the prerequisites for this sort of enjoyment: in a quiet old age, not so far away now, spent more or less immobile between fireside and garden, I hope to watch the panorama of the world I have loved so much spread out for me by other eyes than mine.

Life in general requires a balanced diet, a variety of ingredients to make it healthy, and books are the easiest means ready to hand for the supplementing of any deficiency there may be. The novel brings its ripple of intercourse for the lonely, and the detective story a few hours of suspense and excitement for those who suffer, perhaps unconsciously, from the paralysis of routine. The travel book opens a new horizon and is the best prescription for all prisoners – and how many of them there are! Not only the inactive, or the sick, but all who are tied down by duty, or riveted to a daily job, however interesting it may be: their diet suffers from constriction.

For them the travel book opens that magic Hans Andersen country, where the two children spread the fairy's little handkerchief before them and could wander through all the landscape of their delight. The thought, that one can share one's pleasure, is one of the most agreeable among the incidents of a writer's labours, and the good travel book should be a genuine companionship, an expedition to be taken up or put down at will but always with the feeling that, in the midst of novelty, one is not alone. For this reason it is the most *personal* of all literary forms except perhaps poetry: through all its vicissitudes, the author is beside you, delightful with odd reflections or prosy with too many small complaints – ailments, dishonest servants, too many breakfasts and dinners and teas: there he is, as he is in real life no doubt, and you feel that you know him very well. 'British officers cannot go wrong in attacking at three A.M ', a statement like this, made apparently without any provocation near some little village on the Asian plateau, could only belong to the period between the Crimean and the first World War; the tough confidence of its age is in it. The same place seen today would start a very different reflection; it is the personal slant of the author that makes or mars the book of travel, and if that is taken away and mere facts are left to stand alone, the thing becomes a guide-book and falls dead.

Travel alone, therefore, is not enough. Even as a documentary it has too many competitors – the picture-books, the Sunday papers, cinerama, television – these also are documentaries and efficient for the work they do, and the innocent elderly man who has 'often thought that my experiences would make a book' (as if books were in the habit of writing themselves) – he who once had a plentiful audience of people interested in his breakfasts in the desert, is now, let us admit it, wholly and unmistakably out of date: the simple jotting down of what happens one day after the other is only to be recommended in such rare far places as are yet unknown: and even these are the better for a few general ideas.

A pattern is required, and the threads of the world are there for the artist's weaving. In that web the strange and the familiar, the trifles of daily life and the immortal search, all colour and all delight, may find their place if he will make of them some intelligible plot. The pattern is what we need.

A consideration of this argument opens up the immense stretches that now divide us from the ages of faith, when a pattern existed ready-made and any facts in which the writer happened to be interested could find a home. Among many other characteristics in the *Divine Comedy* for instance, one is struck by its extreme tidiness; the circles and separations, from deepest hell to heaven, are all well defined and, if one may say so, geometric. This was not Dante's invention; it was the air he breathed, the climate of his time, and his own invention is what he fitted into the existing compartments.

In our age there is nothing so universally acknowledged. The stray facts we gather have no natural place in which to fall and – as the number of them is unmanageably great – we are in danger of being smothered by their impact. The pattern becomes essential, and in the absence of a general standard, every author must provide his own. In a novel this can, and indeed should, be done unobtrusively by the selection of the incidents and the building of the plot; but in travel books, or in history for that matter, the plot is there already, chaotic as a rule and shapeless, and it is the angle at which the author sees it that must bring out its meaning and create its form. The reader, it seems to me, should be left in no doubt as to his direction, for he is to travel with his author and should see where he is going: geography alone is no longer the rule even in Asia, whose actual facts between the Balkans and Japan are known almost everywhere. I remember when I reached Simla how the valleys and the Himalayan spurs seemed to shrink when someone offered to take me to Kula in a car. I had toiled over those distances in my heart all through my childhood with Kim and the Red Lama as a guide.

More and more then, as I see it, the travel book is becoming an interpretation; sometimes of physical things like mountains or plants, to be climbed or collected, or of human relations, or art, or any other aspect of the various world; while the handing on of promiscuous fact, which made the charm of the earlier travellers, is degenerating into the travelogue or that ruthless journalistic art which skims a country in three weeks without an inkling of its language.

Perhaps even in the old days, when facts were still strange enough to be worth telling, the personal angle behind them counted for more than one would think. Curzon and Kinglake and Doughty, Darwin and Layard, all in their different realms, present the landscape they wandered in with a strong slant of their own; and it is this, as well as their gift of observation, which lifts their writing to greatness. For the travel book is *a method for seeing new places with companionship*; and the choice both of places and companions is very wide. One may set out with an entomologist or a historian, or with someone whose eye is on present politics, or one with machines or ideologies to sell; there is in fact nearly always a bias of some sort that makes the writer travel at all. But apart from this, yet penetrating it on all sides, are the two requisites that must be shared by writer and reader, the bond as it were between them: they must both be inspired above all things by curiosity and pleasure, and that will enable them to enjoy earth and its accidents for their own sake, untormented by any wish to interfere.

In a world that grows more governessy every day, it cannot be stressed too strongly that the travel writer or reader must *never* be nagged by the desire to interfere. To the writer this axiom is soon made obvious if he goes to any of the more remote or interesting places: if he tries to interfere he is soon reduced to the impossibility of travelling there at all. But the reader too is disqualified for his full enjoyment if he does not leave preconceived principles behind him, relish the places and people he meets not because they are like him but because they are different, and find them happy, human and often admirable in spite of this disqualifying fact. The reader does indeed possess one great advantage over the actual traveller, and more especially over anyone bound, by some mission or office, to come into more than a fleeting relation with the countries he visits: the rubs and struggles and discomforts are softened when the book comes to be written, or at any rate they can be remembered with equanimity over a cosy fire in one's room. That litany of sorrows over food and transport and disease, over 'the insolence of office' and the spurns whether of merit or demerit, patient or not, that are as eloquent in the Jerusalem pilgrims of the Middle Ages as in the lorry-hiker today; that gloomy hour before dawn, or at the footsore end of the day, when every traveller has asked himself with wonder whether really he is doing this thing for pleasure, and usually makes a mental resolve – regularly broken – that never, never, never will he set out again: all this the reader is spared. The sharpness has indeed departed even from the writer's mind with the first good hour or pleasant meeting, long before he sits down at his table to write: and his memory may be compared to that of widowers who after fifty years of nagging think of the dear one in a rosy glow. In both cases, the memory is probably nearer the actual truth than were the pin-pricks of the moment; but however this may be, the reader of the book is spared all such transitions: prisoner as he is to his office, his health, his family, his poverty, or all the thousand shackles of his days – within the pages of the book he has a freedom greater than that enjoyed by its author, and he can move about there unconstricted by all the agonies of human weakness that beset the actual traveller on his way.

Freedom is the travel book's secret. For some people, accustomed mostly perhaps to the open air, it is a quality so necessary that fife itself is slight in comparison, and they will set out and make their actual journeys. But for most human beings it is one among a number of other ingredients of equal weight, and for these the travel book is written. To both categories in their varying measure the world's landscapes are open and they can wander, and at last perhaps reach the conclusion that the real freedom lives in one's own heart, in its capacity to find in all human variety the basic unity, and the happy acceptance of adventure as it comes.

1957

On Travelling with a Notebook

I was walking, when the first Cyprus crisis was at its height, among the narrow byways that hug the Athens Acropolis, when three or four very small boys came round a corner and asked me where I belonged, naming one country after another. Having exhausted all they could think of, they looked at me with horror when I said, *'Anglia,'* English. The eldest reached for a stone and they all in chorus cried, '*Kyprus.*' Not knowing any Greek with which to argue, I took the first historic name that came into my mind and said, 'Pericles.' The classic bond held. 'Themistocles' one little boy responded, and I added 'Alcibiades' for good measure. The little group instantly adopted me and shepherded me through all the dangers of their fellows, just out from school. This is years ago now and I had forgotten the episode until I happened to read the single word *Anglia* in a notebook of that day and the whole picture with its fierce gay little figures and the Acropolis hanging above them came back into my mind. The notebook, with its single word, had saved it from total oblivion.

A pen and a notebook and a reasonable amount of discrimination will change a journey from a mere annual into a perennial, its pleasures and pains renewable at will.

The keeping of a regular diary is difficult and apt in most lives to be dull as it plods through good and bad at one even pace. But the art of the notebook is selective.

One's, own sensations and emotions should be left out, while the *causes* that produced them are carefully identified. These are usually small concrete facts not particularly spectacular in themselves, and a single word, as we have seen, may recall them. In describing Venice or Athens for instance, it is useless to record the rapture: no mere mention can renew it: but the cause – some shimmer of light or shadow, some splash of the flat-prowed gondola as its crest turns a corner, or a sudden vignette, or the Greeks reading their morning papers in the theatre of Dionysius – such concrete glimpses produced the delight in the first place and can recapture it in the notebook's pages. Colours, odours (good or bad), even apparently irrelevant details like the time of day, are far more evocative than a record of feelings, which represent the writer and not the scene and are, usually, a mere embarrassment in later reading.

I have notes for instance of the Persian tribes moving to their summer pastures under the great tombs of their kings at Naksh-i-Rustum: the tumult of goats, camels and horses, the women's black turbans, the clanking of cooking-pots tied to the saddle, and some effect of dust and distance are jotted down; and the remembrance of that wide freedom, the immensity of the background in space and time, come back automatically with the mention of the sights that caused them.

A painter once told me how important it is in a quick sketch that the few details one has time for should be put in with particular care; far from being less precise they should be more so, or the illusion of reality will fail. The same rule applies to notebook jottings. A painter like Edward Lear shows the same awareness in his diary as in his sketches, where the details of light and colour for which he had no time are scribbled in pencil at the side.

In poetry the process is fundamentally the same, but is worked out more completely with the harmony of words. The everyday traveller's notebook stops short of this process: it is intended for himself alone, it touches a chord already familiar to him, and therefore need not concern itself with the facilities of language: it is reminiscent, not creative, and can be brief and quite unreadable. With a little practice in selection, a very few lines will hold the gist of a whole day's journey; and the writing of them is much less of a labour than one would suppose.

You can amuse yourself too by reversing the process when you are reading. Pick out of any particular description the concrete things the author must have seen and remembered: they have an immediate and convincing authenticity. The psalmist's hills in the mirage of noon that 'skip like lambs' – have we not seen them at the deserts' edges? – or Keats's musk rose 'the murmurous haunt of flies on summer eves'.

From things seen and remembered the fancy soars into the abstract and wanders beyond the notebook's scope – though sometimes even there a simile or image may well be recorded: 'wine-dark' one may fancy the young Homer writing, on some Aegean headland while his sight still held. No confines to the human thought have yet been recorded. But the notebook is not the patrimony only of the thinker: it is an 'Open Sesame' for every holiday traveller who learns to select his adjectives carefully and pack them compactly, so that at any odd moment he may recapture the spell of his days.

1954

The Travel Essay

There are not very many travel essays and few of what there are are worth remembering. The modern travelogue packs a great deal of information into a short span, but it is in the nature of a documentary and can hardly ever be considered as literature; and the essay that can be read for pleasure on its own merits alone very rarely deals with travel except as an accessory – to history, or meditation or any other pursuit that happens to fit more easily than travel into the essay form.

The first thing therefore is to find out why the variety and amusement of travel so seldom suit the essay. And this is not, I think, very difficult to discover.

The essence of travel is diffuse. It is never there on the spot as it were, but always *beyond*: its symbol is the horizon, and its interest always lies over that edge in the unseen. The good travel books can be as diffuse as you like, they are indeed usually the better for being so. Once you have your reader with you, you can take him slow or fast, you can stop to ponder on this or that by the wayside, or hurry him to your inn, or take him off the track altogether in byways of your own; you can be interrupted by a thousand conversations and dawdle the days away with wayfaring gossip; and it is not even essential to bring him to any very definite conclusion at the end: what *must* be done, however, is to bring into the travel book the space and leisure of the journey, there must be no obvious constriction to remind the reader that he is really imprisoned between two boards of cardboard or morocco – he must feel as free as the journey that is described.

Now the essence of the essay is the very opposite of diffuse. It is more like a sonnet in its condensation, with laws of its own just as rigid though less visible; it has to economize its space and therefore, if you were to draw a graph, you would see it go up very sharply to its climax, however gently this abruptness may be disguised. It can of course contain quite a number of ideas and pictures, but they must be related to each other, like a star-cluster rather than the traveller's wandering planet, that rises and moves across the sky and disappears. No mere thimbleful of prose can capture more than a moment here and there of such a traverse, and it is a fact that most of the good travel essays are static; they give their impression of places by singly chosen glimpses of space or time.

Within these limits the essay is an excellent medium for the showing of some vignette or landscape in a high-light of its own; and a great number of travel books and some of the best are really built with essays strung together. Norman Douglas was a past-master in this art, and *Siren Land, Old Calabria*, and *Fountains in the Sand* all give the essence of South Italy or North Africa in a series of luminous snapshots, each of which does nevertheless require the support of its neighbours. Among Middle Eastern books with which I am familiar, Gertrude Bell's *Persian Pictures* may be quoted; each of its miniature studies is in itself quite stationary, some scene of the daily life of the time in Teheran; but the cumulative effect is one of movement – light and shadow and remoteness; and the result is one which no single essay could achieve. This form used in a cumulative way has the great advantage that it allows the author to eliminate the uninteresting stretches of his journey. (I am incidentally often surprised by the – now rather old-fashioned – tendency in travel authors to begin their accounts at their very doorstep, so that the reader is wearied by the whole of Europe before he gets properly started on anything more remote.)

One of my favourite books of this kind is John Addington Symonds's *Italian Sketches*. In his case, the theme chosen for each essay is usually historical, but so enhanced with landscape and with so much interweaving of his own, that the impression is one of movement, with a richly civilized companion, at leisure in the varied beauty of the smaller Italian cities which he loved. He refers to them, in the essay on Monte Oliveto, in words that might be taken to summarize his own delicate and complicated art – 'assigning its proper share to natural circumstances, to the temper of the population, and to the monuments of art in which these elements of nature and of human qualities are blended. The fusion is too delicate and subtle for complete analysis; and the total effect in each particular case may best be compared with that impressed on us by a strong personality, making itself felt in the minutest details. Climate, situation, ethnological conditions, the political vicissitudes of past ages, the bias of the people to certain industries and occupations, the emergence of distinguished men at critical epochs, have all contributed their quota to the composition of an individuality which abides long after the locality has lost its ancient vigour.' Having laid this firm foundation with his reader, his essay finds itself among the famine-stricken citizens of Siena in the year A.D. 1557, when they were handed over to the tyranny of the Grand Duke Cosimo de' Medici; since when, he remarks, 'this town has gone on dreaming in suspended decadence'.

This is extremely competent art, for it eliminates the barrier of Time: past and present are so intermingled, that the essay reproduces the exact mixture a cultured traveller would feel in the century-worn street of almost any small Italian city, whose modern life is cradled in its past. If anyone wishes to test the skill of this writing he need only compare it with W. D. Howells, for instance – another writer of the end of the nineteenth century who takes us wandering through the Italian cities, but without ever making us forget that we are listening to *his* journey and are not there on our own account. This is due partly to the fact that his personal reminiscences are rather dull in themselves, but also to a technique not suited to the essay: he is trying to tell us all he knows about the place, instead of leading up, as Addington Symonds does, in a leisurely but determined way to one particular climax.

It is useful, I think, to compare the essay with the sonnet. Neither of them is intended for general description; they are flashlights directed to one point. The sonnet has the extreme rigidity of literary form: its first eight lines introduce the subject, and the following six deal with what the poet has to say about it; and the invisible structure of the essay, though the same in principle, is much freer in its distribution. In both forms, however, if a general description is intended, the same device is used: the form is kept unbroken, and the feeling of continuity is produced by a *sequence* of sonnets or a *collection* of essays; the single specimen of either is not suited to describing continued motion in space or time.

Take, for instance, one of the most descriptive of Shakespeare's sonnets:

> Full many a glorious morning have I seen
> Greeting the mountain tops with sovereign eye, . . .

Its first eight lines follow, from morning to night, the journey of the sun; but this is merely to prepare the point of sharp and solitary observation at the end. Any prolonged development has to be given by a sequence, such as Shakespeare's own, or Meredith's *Modern Love*, or many others. Both the single sonnet and the single essay deal only with one short view out of a window, though it may be, and often has been, a casement opening on the faery foam.

*   *   *   *   *

Bearing all this in mind, and supposing that We have no time to write either a book or a collection, how do we set about to bring into the compass of our essay as much of the travel magic as we can?

We begin, or at least I do, by recalling the moments or events that roused some feeling, good or bad. But having remembered these moments, without which basis of emotion nothing can come to life, we are careful not to record them, but to continue to look with memory or notebook into the background that produced them. The emotion itself was a result – it was the end of the adventure, and made its way into our private universe and stopped there; and whatever words we use can never bring it to life again, in other minds: but the thing that caused it, whether sight of landscape, or meeting with people, or a clutch of fear – whatever the incident, it still has the power to arouse its own sensations, if it is livingly described. This is no easy task, for it requires practice to disentangle in the first place what it was that struck home among the crowded elements of even the simplest occurrence, and in the second place to find the words that fit. Two accuracies are required, and the first and most difficult is the accuracy of thought.

To look back over journeys and so dissect their moments is a useful and beguiling occupation, whether one intends to write or no. With the hook of its emotion to recall us, the slightest event – so long as it once held us – can regain its lustre and live. I remember, for instance, with a strange sharpness after many years, coming upon a chained bear along a Turkish road. He was being led along by some gipsies and I can now realize that what went to my heart was the slack and drooping chain, which meant that rebellion was useless and his struggles for liberty were over; perhaps that, and some human implication in the long road and the sagging shoulders, and the dust that padded, the bleached fur that must have been sleek and shining when he was a young bear in the roadless hills. I did not disentangle this at the time, for I like to enjoy the day's journey without troubling to investigate till the evening or the next day or two come with their notebook – and this I think is in any case advisable, since it allows an interval for the events to take their place: the *feeling* that they have aroused then brings them more or less sharply before us, and we can hand them on to others by recording – not the feeling itself – but the carefully discovered facts which caused it.

This maxim applies to all writing, and in a supreme way of course to poetry. Wilfred Owen's *monstrous anger of the guns* clutches at any heart that has heard the guns in war: the observation reconstructs what lies behind the emotion.

But for the traveller's essay the recapture of reality is not enough. Having collected the events he wishes to describe, he is only at the beginning of his troubles, for he has to contract them into his narrow frame. No mountain range, no *Alps from end to end*, but one peak alone is he advised to deal with, and as this contradicts the very essence of travel – that is of motion from point to point – he has so to arrange his material that the actual journey becomes a secondary consideration. This is why the best travel essays are centred round something – history, natural history, a personal philosophy, anything in fact – that is not strictly travel and allows the theme of movement to escape as it were beyond the essay's bounds.

The conclusion, my readers may feel, and they would not be far wrong, is that I do not think of the essay as a very good form for the travel story, though anything can be done by anyone if they are skilled enough. I should like, for instance, to read essays on travel by Lawrence Durrell who seems to me to have this century's supreme gift for the truthful and inspired evocation of landscape. As a personal literary pastime, however, and apart from any thought of publication, the travel essay cannot be improved upon. Not everyone, after even the most entrancing journey, is prepared to sit down and write a book; but many people must feel that they would like to fix some moments for their future enjoyment, and this, the mere writing – or even the attempt at writing – their essay will do. They will see that the simplest occurrences were not accidental black or white as they had imagined, but infinitely subtle preparations of which only the final result came to impinge upon their travelling eye; and when they have delved carefully into this background of all that made them think or feel during their journey – they need not bother to write their essay after all, for their memories, so accurately fixed, will not betray them.

1965

Travel in Africa and Persia and the Cyclades goes on through two essays of reminiscence to make its way, one hopes, towards that quieter detachment that may look back on Time. This ticking clock is ever in our ears, and beyond it is the untranslatable silence. The strangeness of age is to walk the narrow ridge between the two – the one is dear and familiar, and the other our promised home. We need have no fear; but since the pleasant vanities of this world are not to last for ever, and the enjoyment of a flowering meadow, or a dress from Paris, or swallows dipping to drink at evening from their pool – since all these enchanting trifles are presumably destined, as far as we are ourselves concerned, to come to an end – we may as well cherish them while peacefully waiting for that greater radiance, and meanwhile try, like the juggler before the altar, to honour them with our words, for our own pleasure and that of others, as best we may.

Tunisia for the Tourist

A small country, manageable in a month's touring; provided with few but all necessary roads, and such as need no four-wheel drive to deal with them, even when it rains; good hotels that have not yet lost the French touch that went to their conception; and an easy distance – a hop across the Mediterranean from Rome. Such is Tunisia. It has other advantages too – a great variety enclosed in a scale of gradations that run from north to south, so that according to caprice or weather one can taste the desert edge at Tozeur or dream away the misty grey-eyed spring among hills that the northern ploughland covers, gentle undulations as green as English downs.

If I were asked what makes a tourist country *par excellence*, I should say that it is the subtle quality which produces in the visitor contentment. This is the opposite of exploration, which stimulates, excites, and often lacerates, but never soothes with that pleasurable quiescence to which the quality of contentment is allied. There must be a certain amount of contentment in any journey, but for the tourist it should be a surface emotion, the ripple of trifles over a background that holds no sudden traps, no darkness at noonday, no rifts to show with unexpected edges the thoroughly unstable substance of our world. One could not, for instance, be a happy tourist in the neighbouring and – geographically – equally agreeable country of Algeria at this time. The turbulence so near its western border at present adds, if anything, to the Tunisian atmosphere of calm.

One of the main elements that produces this atmosphere is the long and varied history of its past.

Unhappy far-off things and battles long ago: Wordsworth's syllables knew the magic and drip the very essence of repose; and in Tunisia this distillation is everywhere apparent. From the time of the pre-historic flints of Gafsa collected by Norman Douglas, the country has been perpetually inhabited, and strange communities in earth-scooped dwellings above the heights of Mareth cannot be living so very differently from their Stone Age ancestors. In their tunnelled hillside rooms scooped round excavated courts open to the sky but invisible to their neighbours, they listened with a feeling of security, they explained, to the explosions when Rommel was fleeing and the Eighth Army pursuing in the defiles below. From those heights the cultivated eastern coastland stretches like a map, its sandy soil drilled with olive rows far out of sight. In their midst, and speaking with the eloquent voice of architecture, the amphitheatre of El Djem tells of an age of rich and sophisticated audiences along those empty seats. At the edge of the sea the towns remain – Gabes and Sfax, Mahdia and Monastir and Sousse. They too had their days, less ancient than El Djem in their heyday; for here the Muslim conquerors of Africa settled their fighting confraternities in castles that combined the properties of monastery, lighthouse and fortress; and from here they set out on the conquest of Sicily and carried on the older tradition of rapine along the north African coast.

It is always surprising how the atmosphere which surrounded a spot at its building will persist through so many vicissitudes and ruins. The inland towns of Roman Tunisia were planned in a comfortable age; small and rich, they looked down from the shallow crook of their hills on to the watered plain that fed them, while they cut up the lovely marbles, the onyx and the green cipollino of their mountains, to build temples and then churches, and always colonnades. Under the same pattern or convention – for the lay-out is much the same in all these little cities – a great deal of rivalry and competition must have existed: one can feel the municipal pulse beating as it were under foundations which the Vandal, or the Berber, or Time have levelled, or blossoming out into some poor forgotten column, chipped ever more carelessly and roughly as the civilization wanes and the ages pass.

Things happened to them. At Thuburbo Maius, for instance, the debased pilasters and a later cycle of habitation squat blindly on the elegant mosaics of the Antonine days. No great interval had elapsed: but when, about A.D. 400, the devastated region was re-peopled, the Vandals had come and gone: the loss of the delicate craft was the price of their reign.

If we knew enough we could read, as in the wrinkles of a face, the writing of many unrecorded sorrows. But the point about the tourist is that he does not know too much. He need not delve into the misery that shifted the ancient columns and built the conquerors' splendid forest of marble for the mosque of Kairouan; enough to loiter there and feel, perhaps without even recognizing it, the blend of all the distant origins that make the difference between a chord and a mere note in the harmony of time. In the Roman sites – Sbeitla and Utica, Dugga and Constantine and others – the note is clearer, the message of a single people shifting from its temples to its churches more or less undisturbed; yet these straightforward communities also are built on a tragic substratum of Punic graves. Little Tophets, where the ashes of sacrificed infants stood in pots beneath triangular stones – they have mostly disappeared; where they exist, one turns with relief to the gentle living of Rome, the paved streets and pleasant courts of the Utica houses, the majesty of the Antonines' Carthage by the sea, and gladly forgets how beastly the Romans were to those poor baby-killers in their day. In Tunis, or in Carthage close beside it, one can see the whole of the western Mediterranean at work from Dido's age to ours; from the little Tophets to the colossal remnants of the Antonine baths and the thistle-strewn apse of the Christian basilica – is it St Cyprian? I have forgotten – the grey of whose aisle seems delicate and perennial as the sea below. We can enjoy the square minarets of the Muslims of the West, with traceries that look like embroidery upon them, and the living Muslim world in the *suqs* below, where women walk swathed in white under whitewashed arcades.

Unlike so many of the Eastern nations today, the people of Tunis are fond of their history; they are restoring and preserving their medieval houses – whose stucco and coloured tiles are in fact extremely beautiful – and one is free to wander, or to take photographs without any ideological interference, in an ancient world within hearing of the Tunis boulevard.

1961

The Golden Domes of Iraq and Iran

The first Holy Cities or places of pilgrimage in the Muslim world were of course Mecca, Medina, and Jerusalem, whose temple-rock still shows the hoof-mark of the Prophet's horse when he left this earth to visit Paradise. Apart from such major sites, the habit of pilgrimage developed chiefly among the Shi'a Muslim. Turning away from the innate republicanism of Arabia, they followed a deeply rooted dynastic tendency in Persia with which the visits to the tombs of saints and martyrs have ever been closely bound: and their great division, still active today, differentiates Persia and one half of Iraq from most of the other Muslim countries of Arabia. Of the Shi'a Holy Cities, Nejf, Kerbela, and Kadhimain are in Iraq, and Qum and Meshed in Persia – the former of these singular in being dedicated to a woman.

The golden dome of Nejf covers the cenotaph of Ali, the Prophet's son-in-law, whose actual place of burial is uncertain; his sons Husein and Abbas lie in Kerbela; Kadhimain and Samarra belong to later descendants in a line of twelve 'Imams' or seven, according to the diverging sects. A family bond unites these holy places: Fatima of Qum was sister to Musa of Kadhimain, and his son in turn lies in Meshed in the holiest place of all, visited by pilgrims from Afghanistan. These tombs are loved and worshipped and all except Samarra are closed to Christian visitors. Their gates and minarets and courts, their coloured tiles and domes – patterned sky-blue or solid gold – belong to many different periods. Most of them have been sacked, destroyed and rebuilt. Their origins are early and were probably very simple – mere open spaces walled like the mosques which the Muslim generals hastened to build in the lands they conquered. The colonnaded enclosures of Cordova, Cairo and Cairowan still show this early pattern: but, in the north and the east, churches were sometimes used; traditions of the church were adopted; and the *domed* enclosures began. There is a tradition that an old onlooker in Jerusalem, watching the great Dome of the Rock as it was being erected, was heard to say: 'We used to build mosques, hut *you* build churches.' The fact is that the masons were conquered Syrians or Byzantines and the conquerors adopted their style; and the Arabic word *qubba*, which means a dome or a tent – and from which our word *alcove* is derived – came to describe the structure that covered a grave.

For many centuries a wall for defence was more important than a dome for beauty, and the modern richness of the Holy Cities, the golden shimmer, is quite recent. Nadir Shah gilded the Nejf dome in 1743, and that of Kerbela was contributed even later by the founder of the Khajar dynasty and redone through the offerings of the faithful, after the disorders of 1801. The faiences of Kadhimain are sixteenth-century, but the gold of its dome is 1870 renewed by Nasr-ed Din Shah; and the early gold of Meshed too was looted, and the restoration of the dome left for a century, to Sulaiman I. For earlier work one must turn away from the gold, to the azure traceries of Isfahan.

The magic of the Holy Cities indeed is difficult now to recapture, since the element that so largely made it was the element of Time. Combustion engines of one sort and another have taken it away: and though the actual view across steppe or desert has not greatly altered, the feeling has changed since those who leave a hotel in Baghdad or Teheran can see the domes of the sanctuaries floating on the selfsame day in their pale skies. Preparation is lacking. The pilgrim, when he walked across those emptinesses that led to his desire – or even if he was rich enough to sway day after day towards it on a camel – had already, as it were, appropriated the golden vision into his dreams. It had been described to him many times in small and remote places by those who had made the long and arduous journey before him. From the Elburz mountains of north-west Iran to Kerbela, or to Nejf in its black walls (now demolished) people, whom I myself have spoken to, have taken a good month on the way. The stages were marked by philanthropic forebears – Zobeide, the queen of the Caliph Harun ar-Rashid, is still kindly remembered. In the desert, by some poor water, at an easy eight-hour or so camel distance one from the other, the square blank walls of the *khans* dissolve with their lonely gateways tumbled in a heap. They gape to empty courtyards where the nights are now solitary and the sun is the only traveller; and the single-storeyed compartments that surround the inside wall, with flattened curves cushioned against the sky – the inner room for the merchant with a door to close it, and the outer pillared space for his own animals to munch beside him within earshot through the night – these too have fallen silent, filled only with the clean and living desert air.

The very name that describes these halting-places tells of a superseded way of travel – they are the *manzils*, the *descendings*, where the load slides from the sweating patch of animal that has borne it since dawn, and the cool pleasure of the evening begins with a few sticks of thorn lighted in a little heap under the samovar for tea. Very recent travellers knew these pains and pleasures – Gertrude Bell, for instance, riding in 1913 out of the sandy belt from the Shammar lands to Kerbela – and knew the sudden lifting of the heart when the golden domes appeared.

The holiest of these, in Iraq, is Nejf, where Ali, the son-in-law of the Prophet, is remembered though his actual death occurred at Kufa near by. There, in a simple mosque walled with a few palm trees in an austere enclosure, he was murdered while he prayed.

In Kerbela, too, violence is recorded under the placid shimmer of the twin shrines. One covers Abbas the half-brother, and the other belongs to Husein, the grandson of the Prophet, who marched from Mecca to claim the heritage of the Caliphs in what he thought would be the friendly country of Iraq. The scene of their death is near by, where the sands begin and the palm trees end near the banks of Euphrates.

This lonely battle opened the long fissure which ever since has separated the world of Islam: the Sunni and the Shi'a. It was a small affair, a continuation of the struggle for the Prophet's inheritance which had already filled the Arab world with wars. In A.D. 680, after his father's murder in Kufa, Ali's son Husein set out with his womenfolk and family and a small devoted band of 30 horse and 40 foot or little more to cross the desert from Mecca. As they drew near Kufa, his father's city, 'each succeeding messenger was fraught with darker tidings'. The bedouin tribes had joined the little band as it travelled through their empty land; but now, seeing the odds too great, they withdrew. One of the chieftains invited Husein to turn aside and wait for a larger force of tribesmen: but 'surrounded as thou seest I am by women and children,' Husein could not turn into the desert: and near Kerbela he was met by the far greater forces of the Umayyad Caliph Yezid.

'The scene that followed is still fresh in the believer's eye: and as often as the fatal day comes round, the 10th of the first month, it is commemorated with the wildest grief and frenzy . . . The fond believer forgets that al-Husein, . . . having broken his allegiance, yielded himself to a treasonable, though impotent, design upon the throne. . . . He can see nought but the cruel and ruthless hand that slew with few exceptions all in whose veins flowed their Prophet's sacred blood.'[1]

Al-Husein obtained a day's respite to send his kinsmen and family away. But they one and all refused to leave him. The tents were rudely staked together, and barricades of such poor wood and reeds as the deserty steppe affords were set around. During the night, the young man's sister heard his servant furbishing his sword and singing, and, drawing her black mantle round her, she stole to his tent through the dark, and beat her breast and face, and swooned. It was little Husein could do to comfort her. They were without water, and with nothing to do but to prepare their scanty weapons through the night. When the morning came, Husein drew out his little force for battle.

'There was a parley: and again he offered to retire, or be led to the presence of the Caliph. Finding all in vain, he alighted from his camel, surrounded by his kinsmen. . . . There was a moment of stillness. At length, one shot an arrow from the Kufan side, and amid the cries of women and little ones, the unequal fight began . . . One after another the sons and brothers, nephews and cousins, fell before the shafts of the enemy. Some took shelter behind the camp. The reeds were set on fire, and the flames spreading to the tents added new horror to the scene. For long none dared attack al-Husein, and it was hoped he might even yet surrender. At last, driven by thirst, he sought the river bank. The enemy closed up, and he was cut off from his people . . . and the cavalry trampled on his corpse.'[2]

It is strange to think of what small numbers the powers that have turned history are so often composed: Thermopylae, for instance, and here this little band who, cut off from water and surrounded by a few sticks of barricade, faced death to the last man. Seventy heads were brought to Damascus and 'the tragedy of Kerbela decided not only the fate of the Caliphate, but of Muhammedan kingdoms long after the Caliphate had waned and disappeared.'[3] Behind it lay two ideologies: the passionate feudalism of Persia climbing tier by tier to its apex of royalty and already well over a thousand years old in A.D. 680 when Husein died; and the deeply rooted, non-dynastic character of the Arab. As one travels about the East today and watches a single pattern of new civilization being offered to people so diverse in their origins and training, some doubt as to a homogeneous result is bound to come. And I may say that a little while ago, soon after the recent killings in Iraq, as I happened at dinner to sit beside a diplomat from that country, I reminded him of the advice that had been given to the Caliph who ruled there when the first tragedy occurred. 'As for Husein', the Caliph's father told him, 'the restless men of al-Iraq will give him no peace till he attempt the Empire; when thou hast gotten the victory, deal gently with him, for truly the blood of the Prophet runneth in his veins.'[4] In this atmosphere, the sacred mausoleums lift up their gold and azure filigree serenely, illuminated through the festival or fasting months of the ages with torches or electric lamps as the case may be, and with, at all times, and however bloody, a constant stream of faith.

When I last went to Kerbela, three years ago, repairs were going on, and the golden bricks of the dome of Husein – each one, they told me, weighed and numbered – had been lifted and replaced. They shone with an incredible softness, like the centre of a rose in the dusty night. The streets too of the Holy Cities have been repaired and widened: their tunnelled shadows that lean at all angles under wooden pillars will soon be cleared away: already an open approach where taxis can circulate before the shrine itself has been engineered in Kerbela and in Kadhimain. Nejf I have not lately seen, but I know that the black wall is down which used to hide it like a sleeping beauty from the desert, its two golden domes alone showing, rounded to a point like breasts. They caught every ray of light for the eye of the travelling pilgrim as the sun wheeled above him and his thirsty steps drew near. Many of these pilgrims were beyond such comfort, for they were dead – slung in coffins or wrapped in folds of cotton, one on each side of a camel, and travelling to rest in holy ground. At the entrance to the town a little building received them, whence, washed and decently prepared, they were carried in open biers round the Mosque of Ali, to be laid in earth nearer or farther, according to what their families could pay. But if you had leisure at the end of your life, or perhaps lacked faith in the piety of your heirs, you would come yourself to join some confraternity of your countrymen and spend these last months or years in meditation, either at your own expense in the family house which many Shi'a Muslims owned from Baghdad or Iran, or else to live on some charitable endowment, in dingy courts off cobbled streets smothered in dust, too narrow between their blank walls for anything on wheels.

The atmosphere of the Holy Cities was different from anything I have known elsewhere. No longer explosive, but like wine long bottled that has gone sour, it poisoned the flavour of life, particularly for the young. Even the breath of the desert, which moves in and out of the bazaars of Baghdad and Damascus, died here on the threshold of those furtive ways. I knew Nejf and Kerbela well, and was – apart from Gertrude Bell, who had known two of them – the only Western woman I believe to be received by the nine or ten *Mujtahids* or Elders who held their little courts of disciples there and ran through their fingers the subtle but superannuated threads that ramified to Iran, Afghanistan, India and far beyond – wherever a Shi'a Muslim lived who once had visited the tomb of Ali. They were all different, and their old heads – alert, kindly, shrewd, or bitter – were draped in turbans of varying fashion: but they all shared an undefinable atmosphere of authority, gained no doubt as they climbed up through the vague and undefined ranges of their power: for there is nothing but the general consensus of opinion to make a *Mujtahid* out of an ordinary man, and he has to rely on such an appearance of austerity as often made me think of the early tales of puritan America – Nathaniel Hawthorn, for instance – with all their pitfalls for the natural frailties of men. The young longed to creep out of this network into the contemporary world; and the happiest perhaps were the poor and the old who, gathered from the corners of Asia, lived round their ark of salvation, in attendance on a future in which their faith was secure.

No tourist, looking down in his fleeting way from some neighbouring roof on to the court of the shrine, can get even an inkling of what this feeling of safety may be. I have visited two of the very holy tombs – Samarra, on the Tigris between Baghdad and Mosul, which is not a Shi'a but a Sunni city, and therefore open to access for those of another faith who treat it with respect; and Meshed in Iran, whose shrine for a very short time during the second World War could be visited while the government of the city and mosque were in the hands of the same man. He was a friend of my friends who were consuls then in Meshed, and he took us through the courts and tiled arcades to where the Imam Ridha sleeps in his massive silver cage beneath his golden dome. But though this is the meeting-place of nearer and central Asia, and the most venerated shrine in Iran, the magic that no doubt lurks there was shattered by our alien visitation. It was rather in the purlieus of the great door of Nejf that I found it, where – hidden and unnoticed behind the smokers of the *qalian* (hubble-bubble) at a little café – I spent many evening hours watching the faithful as the winged arch swallowed or rejected them under its rose-patterned tiles. To sit there among the pressed houses, so crowded within the security of their wall that there was scarcely room in front of the mosque for a little stone-flagged square, was to realize what for several thousand years of our history has constituted the *feeling of safety*, the close-packed enclosure of small cities crammed within walls. Outside, are the wilderness, or the neighbouring unfriendly cities, or the raiding deserts; inside, the intimacy where strangers or dissenters are watched with fear or anger. And from the outer suburbs that swell or shrink in times of peace or war, this intimate sense of safety and seclusion grows and grows – through the dark bazaars, and the taller clustering houses, through the courtyard, and into the last inner sanctity of the shrine itself. To enter here was, when I lived in Iraq (and still is, I believe) forbidden, and I have done so only once and at some danger, in disguise, in a night of Ramadhan.[5] Thousands of black-veiled women were walking about in the lighted court under the gold, with a buzz like a hive in its shadows, and it was only after passing through them, through the heavy doors under their stalactite alcoves, through the halls in their jumble of bric-à-brac and splendour, to the tomb itself in its cage polished by hands of prayer, that the passion became tangible as it were – the passion that had brought so many weary feet across the wastes of Asia.

This fierce feeling of safety and exclusion melts into what we think of as civilization when we leave the Holy Cities of Iraq or Persia and step under the azure domes of Isfahan. Those lovely mosques were built or renovated in an easier and an opulent age among a people where the Shi'a form of Muhammedanism was universal, instead of being held as in Iraq by an unencouraged population in antagonism with its rulers. The Persian love for the ornaments of life pierces through religion in the domes of Shah Abbas; mistily lost in their blue patterns, they melt above our heads like flights of birds into an atmosphere part heaven and part the pale Iranian spring. The seasons of this world are ever remembered: in the *Masjid-i-Shah* the 'Royal Mosque' at the bottom of the oldest polo ground that is now the open space of Isfahan, the four *liwans* (the covered spaces) are built for the four seasons, one by an artist from Kerman, the other three by Isfahanis; the differences of their carpets are visible in the patterns of their domes. Here everything has mellowed; the foreign visitor is welcomed at all except the hours of prayer, and the temper of meditation rises from its sectarian hedges into the air of peace. Walking there under the building of the craftsman, 'the humble one, the Servant of God, the Isfahani, who requires your prayers', one thinks of mosques and tombs scattered over Asia, fragments of a splintered turquoise sky that covers the Muslim world. Whether it is the new mosque with its shops clustered like chicks under a hen in the High Street of Baghdad; or the ruined splendour of Tabriz built by converted invaders; or the lonely chapel on an arid ridge of some forgotten saint – the whole lightness of the landscapes of Asia is centred, when one comes to think of it, on these fanciful, diversely decorated symbols of enduring faith.

1961

Lunch with Homer

The Cyclades lie crumpled and easy on the glass of the Aegean, scoured by empty defiles that produce no more than some fever-spurt of torrents in the spring. Almost treeless, but seamed like skeleton leaves with goat-walls long since built to save forgotten vineyards, their paths are thinly scratched, the poverty of their harvests is fleeting and uncertain, and Time has fingered every disintegrating precipice and furrow. From any high point of vantage, the little waves that skim the noonday water show their triangular shapes and useless hurry as they trip under the *melteme* towards the shores; and the deep implacable blue is fringed with a gossamer wreath of air, a white illusion, round all the island bases.

The sun transforms these islands as he sinks. The air turns from white to azure like an opening hyacinth along the horizon, enveloping them in its invisible curves. Their dryness and hardness and all their detail disappears, and their villages shine for a moment until they too are smoothed into the tideless evening, while the sun's last slabs of gold flatten the sea. The *melteme* dies soon after noon and the waters' lucid edge now scarce turns over to write its hieroglyphs along the beaches; and only the high island outlines, free as it Were of their pedestals, are left to flash like a shoal of fishes in the last of the sun.

Their fierce history is sunk below in shadows more opaque than those of the gathering night, and the tourists are safe in their lodgings along the small bits of boulevarded shore; and in the upper villages the lights that are friendly with darkness, the oil-lamp and cooking fire, still appear to gather rather than to pierce the twilight, as they have done through the long wildernesses of their past. With his day behind him, the fisherman or muleteer sits on the whitewashed wall of his village and looks out over headlands, diminishing one beyond the other till shadows fold them in a last Orphic embrace in which they die.

This visitation of beauty, this daily miracle as regular as the light and shade of their toil or the water in the clefts of their rocks, perhaps gives to the islanders their cool transparent gaze. Their life has moulded them, through an austere and kindly village childhood and the poverty of youth and rub of middle years, till in their old age one sees them rugged and sifted down, like eagles grown gentle, with the sunlight of their days still in their eyes. Their age is respected, for it is no small acquisition out of the rigour of their labour, and an old man can sit on his doorstep or even on a chair and command any young one around to offer whatever delicacy is in season, figs or grapes or apricots, to the wayfarer on his hill; and with his bleached clothes and stubbly chin and hands furrowed and ridged and sunburnt like the rocks around him, can look every day into the ineffable face of Beauty, which has been with him so long that it is now inside him, and he does not even know that it is there.

I keep one such island in mind and withhold its name because I like to think of it as private. When I left it last year nothing could run on wheels there although a boulevard is now threatened along its sandy shore; even then, at its southern end, a few miles of road, dusty under bus or lorries, connected its small harbour with the village capital, scooped out of rocks under the highest hill. This is now called St Elias, but once belonged to Helios the sun-god, and his chariot still seems nearer than most things as it travels over the solitude of wind-flattened stones and thyme. One can ride on a mule along the backbone of the island, four hours or so under Elias's shoulder, to the northern end, where no roads, except for mules, exist.

There is nothing here except a small square hotel, a smaller church, a handful of houses on a whitewashed street, and three white villages that look down from their landscape above. A quay with a windmill out of action – now left to satisfy the tourist – shelters five fishing *caiques*, whose subdued creaking or rubbing against each other, or sudden slapping like wet sheets in a wind, spreads news of the *melteme* through the night. There was a time when the *caiques* would creep out with the first breeze as silent as the dawn, but they all now have second-hand engines which make as much noise as the *Dies Irae* in a requiem and spur the laziest tourist to step on to the balcony of his room and look at the sunrise: when this is over and the boats are off, he can sleep again through the peace of the morning.

In 1687, Mr Bernard Randolph reports this island as having been

'formerly very well inhabited, having two towns and ten villages, but in the last Warr betwixt the Venetians and Turks it is much dispeopled, . . .and the Privateers are so continually plaguing them, that Poor Souls, they have not sufficient to pay their tribute . . .To the South is a high mountain, on which there is a sentinel to give notice, if they see any ships coming from the North or Southland they are soon out upon their backs.'[1]

The Italians and the Renaissance persisted in the Cyclades long after the Crusades were over, and there was a court at Naxos, with intrigues and festivals that flashed in and out among the poverties of the islands: but the memory has come down thin and pastoral, a hard survival amid rocky hillsides and the thorny, scented thyme. The place is remembered where a shepherd lad was seized by the Turks and killed while he played his flute to warn his village; a great boulder marks the spot; and white shrines or monasteries plastered almost windowless against unscalable cliff faces still carry their tightrope atmosphere of safety and danger. But these voices have become small and dry, dusted over by a century or more of everyday toil that a man can deal with and put the unexpected out of mind. The origins of memory are anyway out of reach.

On the 15th of August our roadstead and its three villages celebrate their *Panagiya* in the hills. The Turkish raiders once destroyed a church there, and the ikon of Our Lady, hidden at the time among the rocks, had been lost and forgotten. Generations later it was found and brought to the nearest village, but escaped by night to its own solitude; and when this had happened several times, the villagers decided to rebuild the vanished church, and mark its feast with an annual pilgrimage, and so they do. Mass is celebrated, and a meal offered to all who come, and the mules climb up or down, one hour or two according to their stabling, carrying pilgrims on hard wooden saddles knotted with cords. The church stands alone among its uplands, where stone is so crowded that even the optimism of the islanders has ceased to hope for a harvest and the thyme has its freedom and looks as if it were the rock itself in flower.

The village streets, where the mules set out, are spotless with white-wash, whose bold fancies decorate every interval of pavement not occupied by steps; its yearly coating over the houses makes them look soft as milk, and whiteness is everywhere, except for little mounds of natural manure which these animals seem to deposit with astonishing frequency: some old woman runs swiftly with a dustpan to collect it for her garden strip that hangs above the cliffs. The mules, with the village girls bunched on top of them gaily dressed and clutching plastic bags, fill the narrow, shallow street from side to side. They take the steps mincingly sideways, or trot down them at the same expert angle to the anguish of unpractised visitors. When they leave the village and reach steeper places, they droop their heads and relax their ears and, pondering between the trickles of loose stones, infallibly choose the easier way before their muleteer comes up to whack them and say 'Hah': and no one who has much to do with them can doubt that they are thinkers, concentrating on their own affairs with that misleading look of philosophic abstraction which is apt to deceive us all.

They halt and move and halt, in a zig-zag line in the sun, high above steps, and trees, and terraces of wheat or vines, to where the church stands in a dip of the hills, white and turquoise with a silvery dome, and a Greek flag running up its pole, and strings of small coloured triangles everywhere. One Mass is nearly over, and those who have been earlier or go in later are sitting under an awning of sacking where seats and chairs have made a café and *ouzo* is offered here and there. The morning goes easily; the little clanking bell which is merely a strip of metal sounds crazily cheerful at intervals, and Time – that precious commodity so stupidly wasted – lies sunning itself in its Mediterranean cradle as if it were a panther asleep upon the rocks.

I wander about and discover a few wizened olive trees near by where a skinned sheep is hanging; two young men are scraping it clean; thirty are to be done, they tell me, their arms red to the elbow, delighted to pause in their task. Over a thousand people are to be fed, and the sheep are cooked, as soon as they are ready, in a copper cauldron on an open fire near the trestles where luncheon will be eaten under a canopy of leaves. What a thing it is to be on holiday! Anyone might think it distasteful to deal with thirty skinned sheep in a morning, but the young men are beaming cheerfulness and out for enjoyment. Round the great cauldron, the buxom girls stir in a swarm; Mass is over; and the *Papas* – a rugged twinkling old man in a frayed black cassock – is out for an interval of gossip; the crowd grows every minute and the long line of mules can be seen winding towards us from far over the hills. Brown earthenware bowls and forks and spoons begin to be laid along the trestle tables, and the first batch is soon let into the enclosure while the rest of us continue with our *ouzos*, or coffees, or sweet paste called *submarine* which the Greeks like to suck with a tumbler of water.

In a strange way it all seems familiar. Where have we lunched like this before? In the Odyssey of course. In Pylos with Nestor and in other places. Prayers and food, landscape so hard as to be almost unchangeable, and holidays in the sun – they slip hardly interrupted through the comings and goings of religions and invasions.

> The ox on broad earth then laid laterally
> They held, while Duke Pisistratus the throat
> Dissolv'd, and set the sable blood afloat,
> And then the life the bones left. Instantly
> They cut him up; apart ran either thigh,
> That with the fat they dubb'd, with art alone
> The throat-brisk and the sweetbread pricking on.
> Then Nestor broiled them on the coal-turned wood,
> Poured black wine on; and by him young men stood,
> That spits fine-pointed held, on which, when burned
> The solid thighs were, they transfix'd and turn'd

> The inwards, cut in cantles; which, the meat
> Vowed to the Gods consum'd, they roast and eat.[2]

The crazy bell pronounced the last Mass over and a steady stream now waited in a queue for their meal. The island's young policeman came to take us in directly as honoured guests to a side-table, where the feast stretched in two long rows of seated eating figures, dappled in sun and shadow under the canopy of leaves. The thirty sheep had been slaughtered close by; the huge copper cauldron's embers were still smouldering and that sweet sticky smell of blood which the Gods so much enjoyed very nearly overcame a mortal like myself – and a degenerate one at that, for no one else seemed to mind. The broth steamed richly up with the 'inwards' inside it; and whatever it was that Nestor had cut up for his guests followed in a second brown earthenware bowl, stewed with potatoes, which are a luxury of the islands.

The village girls carried round amphorae of *rezina*, poured with a classic gesture from the crook of the arm – that, too, how long remembered! And when the meal was ended, large trays came to collect what contributions everyone could afford. The island feast, so gay in its solitude, was over for the year, though there would still be village dancing in the evening.

The afternoon was already turning to those apricot colours that show the end of daylight on the rocks, and the mules were taking their charges briskly homeward, their muleteer swinging some leg-of-mutton, uncooked and left over, as he strode behind them. I made my way over the smooth worn stones that look so easy and are so deceitful, and thought of the accumulated memories which go back farther than the single memory of men. By their help we are lifted like children on the shoulders of the ages, to think ourselves wiser than our forebears and look on landscapes which they never saw. We think of this background as a shackle, and indeed it is often allowed to be so: yet I have seen too many slow-built harmonies broken by alien invasion and – peaceful or otherwise, and whatever the eventual result may be – a period of great anguish and weakness must ever mark the change. Those are fortunate for whom their luck or wisdom, or geographic circumstance, keep the new values in the same general direction as the old, remembered or forgotten. They lunge into their future like a boxer in the ring; for the punch of a man's strength is not in his fist alone, but in the whole body of his past that makes him what he is.

1967

Passing Fashions

In north Italy, among the foothills where I live, one can see peasants driving their ox-carts home under a load of hay, or grapes, or faggots, according to the season of the year. The oxen sway towards each other, as if they were resisting invisible buffets of air in the calm valley, and the long shallow carts creak and groan in the joints of their axles, as rheumatic as the peasants who still attend to this old-fashioned labour while young men drive the tractors and belong in general to the age of the machine.

The old ox-cart has had a long run through history from when it first came with solid wooden wheels from the nomad steppes of Asia, and its day is nearly over. Looking down upon it with a friendly fellow-feeling, I sometimes think of how many things I have myself seen fading into the forgetful past, and go over them in my mind, wondering at the strange human capacity we carry with us for surviving as it were ourselves.

Figures I can remember belong to an almost fantastically medieval world, like the old Italian nobleman who for years wore a hair-shirt (an animal fur I gathered) as a pious discipline next his skin, and was admired – though not imitated – when he died. Even then, about sixty-five years ago, he was an anomaly, and we lived in what might now be called with our modern arrogance an underdeveloped neighbourhood (as if everything were not underdevelopment this side of eternity). We were backward, anyway, and I can still hear, in my mind, two old market women criticizing the sandals my sister and I rather dashingly wore: 'Poor children,' they were saying, 'there must have been an illness, and their parents made a vow to keep them barefoot if they recovered.' Another striking medieval touch I noticed in my childhood was the one finger-nail worn long by the municipal clerk in our village to show, I was told, that he belonged to the people who do no manual labour. A detail of this sort sets its mark on a whole epoch of history and change.

The Italian post offices at that time provided little perforated jars filled with a sort of emery sand for the convenience of writers of telegrams, since the blessed invention of an ink that dries quickly had not yet been made; and we used to treasure English blotting-paper, because it was the only kind that left no hideous blob. The pens were steel and apt to get rusty, and my father used a goose quill; he would trim it with a pen-knife, and this pause in the squeaking as it moved along the paper would let us children know when it was safe to interrupt. Such trifles are as idle as that thin line of débris one can scarce call wreckage that lies along the sea-beach, yet they are left by civilizations in their destinies of change. Every wave of invention scatters some of them along the shore. Nausikaa probably did her washing much as I have seen the women do, on a flat stone or thin wooden board at the edge of a stream; and if the washing machine had been invented in her day, she and Odysseus would never have met. There are of course pros and cons to almost every invention.

The motor-car has brought the most revolutionary changes in my lifetime from the point of view of everyday affairs. It has scattered into limbo all sorts of quaint conveyances I think of with affection – the dog-cart on its two high wheels that required a certain agility in mounting with a young horse in the shafts anxious to be off after a feed of corn: the mild little governess cart that could seat six children facing each other, and allowed them to climb out and in at the back without stopping, to ease the round-bellied pony up a hill: the grander equipages, so beautifully sprung, nodding like flowers, that brought afternoon callers under big straw hats, with skirts that picked the dust off the ground as they moved. I came upon one such, still functioning in a suburb in Turkey, and suddenly realized that it was no mere conveyance, but a whole way of life trotting so easily under the flowering apricots behind their garden walls.

There were omnibuses I can just remember in London, held in by an impatient driver with a flurry of horses in front, when I was small enough to be lifted in at the back. As I grew up, the motor-car was there, but not in full possession: it had captured the bus, on whose deck seats one could now sail with a delightful feeling of freedom and the risk of a shower; but open carriages still trotted round Hyde Park on a Sunday morning, and a funereal 'growler' would take one with one's luggage to the station; and if one were rather emancipated, a hansom cab would come at a whistle from the young man who would see one home after a party, side by side with Romance through the empty gas-lit streets. To whistle for a cab was not, I was told, a thing for a well-brought-up girl to do; like many other maxims of the time, it presupposed that there was always a man around to look after one.

All these phantoms have clip-clopped away into limbo, and it some-times seems strange to me that theirs was the world I lived in and felt much as I do now. The present, while it holds us, we think of as permanent, and are apt to look on every fashion as fluid except our own. In the matter of transport, the age to which I belong is that of the railway: I still welcome its limited freedom of movement, its views of landscape solitudes unencumbered by roads or houses, as the normal atmosphere of travel. When I can, I find a not-too-rapid train that trun-dles through easy country and stops (not too long) at wayside stations; and this gives me a feeling of leisure, and comfort, and the habitable nature of the world; but this too, I know, is well upon its way, and even the Orient Express, most splendid of trains in its period, already has a tarnished look; its *wagon-lit* attendants, recognizing no doubt the railway age of their passenger, come up to greet me with the air of one refugee welcoming another.

Heat and light come after transport in the importance of their changes through my time. The bath, so lamentably treated by Christianity, is only now coming back into its own, and was a poor but agreeable affair in my childhood, a round tin receptacle placed on a warm white blanket in front of the bedroom fire. Its pleasure depended on the general warmth of the room (which I would now think full of draughts) and on the toys one was given to play with; and it had the human sociability which modern comfort tends more and more to exclude, and which marks, it seems to me, the chief difference between that old world and the new. In the absence of gadgets controlled by switches, everything one did required the presence of some human being or animal to help in the doing, and made an intricate and varying pattern, a jig-saw into which one's own little angular shape had to fit. No fire could burn without someone to light, sweep, or lay it, and the great red glow of the kitchen range itself behind its iron bars was unthinkable without Cook somewhere in the vicinity, benevolent or short-tempered according to the progress of her dinner.

The same assiduous service entered into the production of light, and the lamp-lighter with his wand in the dusk, flitting under lamp posts so that they blossomed like urban flowers in his trail, made the legend of Prometheus as understandable as if we had belonged to the first twilights of the human world.

The Greeks, when the Persians had been vanquished and the invasion was over, purified their altars and desecrated lands with fire, and this sacred feeling came down, unrecognized but probably potent, to my day. A long row of oil-lamps had to be cleaned and trimmed every morning by the daughters of the house, not from any hieratic motive, but because our rather rough servant girls seemed unable to carry out the delicate operation successfully; and though I took a strong dislike to oil-lamps which kept me an hour or two indoors on fine summer mornings, they no doubt encouraged feelings of respect and awe with which I have sat by many a later camp-fire as it fell to its embers in desert nights. The whole of my generation watched as it were the taming of fire, from the tree-branch burning on its open hearth to the electric switch in everybody's bedroom. The interval was bridged by gas, which sizzled cheerfully above ornamented brackets in Edwardian drawing-rooms, and blackened the paint so that it had to be renewed every few years. When electricity came, and the powers of water and fire worked together for the benefit of mankind, it was natural to be optimistic and to think of a world swiftly emerging into Light.

It is mortifying perhaps, though I do not find it so, to think how much our lives are affected by the coming and going of material objects. The cut-throat razor, for instance: it needed constant sharpening on a strip of thick leather, and its use was a minor art and one of those that make one admire the pertinacity of mankind since the damage done to oneself while learning them must be so great. The visible effect of the safety-razor was the appearance at breakfast of people with many little gashes on their faces stopped with cotton wool. There are few modern inventions – apart from those in medicine and dentistry – that I think of as *unqualified* benefits, but the safety-razor is, I should say, one of them.

If one begins to think of it, the scope of quite a small mechanical invention is able to throw a historic shadow entirely out of proportion to itself, and history is a catalogue of these beginnings and endings – the Greek phalanx pitted against the Roman sword, or the Spanish Armada defeated not only, I have been told, by the weather, but by the English construction of a sea-proof trap-door, which allowed them just in time, (for once) to place their guns amidships more steadily than the high-pooped Spaniards were able to do. Such fascinating trails pursue their passing fashions beyond the object and its disappearance, through influence after influence on character and life, till they fade into the very boundaries of Time. The dark side of the motor-car for instance is not so much its noise, smell, and creation of ugly straight roads with even more ugly pill-boxes for petrol, but the fact that it has practically deprived our bodies of the normal human activity of walking, with all the changes that this does and will entail.

In following the inventions and fashions of my day as far as a single experience can do so into their immaterial suburbs, their general pattern seems to me fairly plain – an easing of life and an increase of leisure, together with a growing difficulty in dealing with these advantages as they come: this feeling is generally recognized by the ardour with which philanthropy and danger and other *extrovert* things are now pursued; we are not, I think, more inclined to these activities than we were when I was young, but the hardness of life in those days brought them as it were to our door, smaller in scale but familiarly involved with us and our everyday affairs. Whatever the advantages of the machine may be – and they are many – the very ease of its use is bound to make away with *intimacy* – the intercourse of human beings, of animals, or of that which we still think of as the natural world.

That kindly and often irritating network helped and surrounded us, and gave what may be our greatest sorrow to lose in the future – a feeling of being at home in the world and its variety. It gave us a small building in which every stone was familiar – pleasures, duties, difficulties, despairs – they are there today, but half of them out of sight or unacknowledged; and the greatest of our coming troubles may well be this crowded solitude of cities. An invention or two is required that is not purely mechanical, and the pleasantest such modern impulse that I notice has nothing to do with machinery, but is in the hands of the boys and girls who marry young and bring up their children with a personal care far more noticeable than what I remember in the Victorian houses of my childhood.

1967

In Defence of Smuggling

On the French-Italian frontier – where I spent some years of my life – the husband of our cook happened to be a smuggler, and would go off on Tuesdays and Fridays with a band of colleagues, each carrying a note of a thousand lire and a thousand francs for the Italian and French gendarmes respectively at the pass of the Alpes Maritimes. To be taken across the frontier either way without a passport cost fifteen thousand lire.

At this time – it was the late 1940's – little boats would put out quite openly in the sunset from Menton or Ventimiglia and wait for a thin shred of darkness to land their goods on one side or the other of the border while the posts on the main road waylaid the more legitimate travellers with infinite delays. Even there, evasions could be engineered. The most ingenious one I heard of was that of a woman with her sick boy whose leg, wrapped in plaster, was to be X-rayed on the other side of the frontier at San Remo. The police had been informed that this was a ruse at a time when gold was being largely smuggled across. They insisted on cutting open the plaster to see, and found nothing but the injured limb.

'What-shall I do?' wailed the tearful mother, as they plastered the leg up again. 'The boy has to go to the hospital every week, and will you open it every time?'

'Never again, Madame: you need have no fears.' She was sent off in a cloud of apology, and able to return for a number of weeks after with her boy's leg lapped in gold to the amusement of both sides of the border.

French Menton was nearer to my home than Italian Ventimiglia and I would carry on a modest little household smuggling of my own in coffee – which was difficult to get in Italy at that time. In my father's day, I would slip an unnoticed parcel into the folds of his burberry pocket and rely on the transparent integrity of his innocence to walk us through; but when I came to be alone, I would hold up my shopping-bag and say 'coffee', relying on the old diplomatic cliché that the best disguise is the truth, and would usually walk on equally unchallenged. The sleepy old guard once came out from his little box and felt the beans through the bag and asked what they were; but it was a hot afternoon, and the siesta hour, and 'You had better not inquire,' said I; and he kindly desisted. They came to know their usual clients, and on one occasion apologized to me for a new official whose zeal over a miserable jar of treacle had made me walk from a subsidiary post in the hills to the highroad: 'He is young,' they excused him. 'He is still attached to the regulations.'

One may notice in the course of a variegated life that illegality need not always be disapproved of. The tolerance with which it is accepted is possibly due to a remote feeling that law is not infallible and human nature has its rights. No one has thought the worse of Shakespeare for poaching. Highwaymen and pirates have enjoyed a measure of sympathy, undeserved I should say, increasing no doubt as their threat diminished and seas and roads became safer. And in the present state of our society, which does its best to think of security as normal, smuggling continues to hold a sort of extra-mural respectability. Men usually dislike it – from cowardice I think and not from virtue – but one may say that almost the whole female sex is addicted to it by nature, and here a psychologist might perhaps find one of the permanent differences between us.

Strangely enough, since I usually belong to the other party, I am personally inclined to side with the police. Perhaps it comes from living so much on borderlands in Asia, where the odds are weighted heavily against them. I have never been able to evade them for long while riding about near a frontier, and when finally caught have felt a sympathy for their hard and poorly rewarded and solitary lives. They eke them out, one must admit, with a rather scanty amount of plunder from the very poor, but their chief support is moral, and comes from Man's simple loyalty, which he produces merely by banding himself with other men and devoting himself to something or someone out of sight. Watching the cheerful endurance and constant hardship of their lives, I came to have a great liking and respect for these tough people, many of them already grizzled in their service, who had to pay out of their own pockets for the horses they rode up and down the solitary lands they kept free from intruders and marauders, and whose best hope was to end up respectably in some remote village, with little but their memories and perhaps the rank of sergeant to keep them warm.

Even in more sophisticated places, one should never forget that a Customs officer is human.

The Mediterranean world south of the Alps, having to steer the ship of civilization through such difficult waters and through so many centuries, has long ago come to terms both with its conscience and with the ups and downs of the Customs officer's character. It is a world that still continues, in spite of every sort of injustice and oppression, to make life livable and pleasant through one millennium after another. Its basic characteristic is, I think, that it has an infinite optimism about human nature. It does not assume that one is wicked because one does wicked things. It goes on being polite through activities that would spell exclusion from clubs in Washington or London; for it recognizes morality, but treats it as a private possession, not to be too much mixed up with the art of living as such. It has seen too many landmarks removed, too many formulas exploded, to believe that there can be an intrinsic difference between the smoking of a cigarette one side of a border or the other. It limits its disapproval to those who are found out.

With any luck, one may be sure that the Customs officer shares these views in his heart of hearts. His life, one must remember, is very boring. We come to him exhilarated by the intriguing variety of our little stratagems and he has the weary task of frustrating them: he is grateful for any flash of interest or amusement. I once spent a long day in the *Dogana* of Venice seeing some trunks of household goods through labyrinths of paper. The trunks were mostly old worn books which

I had thought of as perfectly easy, but it appeared that all literature required a permit from the Ministry of Interior before being allowed into Italy. The hours passed while this hurdle was being negotiated, and as I sat there on a hard chair thinking things about bureaucracy, a minor official passing by said pityingly: 'We make you suffer, Signora. We are all scoundrels, we people of the *Dogana*.'

'Well, not all of you,' said I, 'because you may remember that St Matthew was a Customs officer.'

This happily inspired remark was handed on; I could hear it passing in an enlivening way down the bleak and empty corridors; and it must have reached the august and private desk of the Chief of Customs, for my permit came through in a matter of minutes, with no intervention from the Ministry of Interior at all.

Books are anyway a headache for the Customs. Many countries still think that corruption comes from outside, and one cannot expect every Customs officer to be erudite. One sympathizes with those who years ago excluded the poems of Ovid as pornographic from the U.S.A. A more recent case happened to a friend of mine landing in Egypt. He had been reading Aldous Huxley's *Grey Eminence* in the aeroplane, and had it taken from him because the Customs official, skipping at random, saw the name of Father Joseph, and concluded that it must be some communist reference to Stalin.

The Customs officer himself however, sometimes, if he likes their looks, will do his best to help his culprits through.

I have not done any serious smuggling myself, apart from taking a large gold-backed primitive madonna across a border for a friend: but I have occasionally in the East had maps for my travels which I did not wish to be deprived of, and kept in a small double-bottomed suitcase which I carried. When the war was over, a friend in Greece asked me to bring three lengths of expensive silk, and I foolishly packed them in the bottom of this case, and was instantly discovered by the Greek who came on board at Corfu. It should be a smuggler's basic rule never to try to deceive a Greek. On this occasion my defeat was watched by the three Mediterranean ladies who shared my cabin; by several stewards and stewardesses lounging there; and by the Customs officer himself and his two *aides:* who all of them with one accord recognized a fellow human being in distress and came to my assistance.

'What is the silk worth?' said the officer, turning to the nearest woman beside him.

'Artificial,' said she, 'a few drachmas to the yard' – a lie which everyone took in the kindly way it was intended.

My friend's evening gowns were whittled down till they were not worth paying for; I was cautioned against the double-based suitcase; complimented the Greek officer on his quickness; and was allowed my three dress-lengths free of charge.

This would probably not have happened north of the Alps. Tancred's mother, in Lord Beaconsfield's novel, anxious for her son's health and distressed at his predilection for the Orient, laments that he will not travel in 'Protestant countries free from vermin': there is a line of demarcation not merely geographic between the Protestant North and pagan South. But the difference is, I think, not one of virtue – a matter anyway hard to assess in a relative world. It is rather due to the increase in the number of things the individual considers to be his own business only as he travels to the south.

If we like individuality – as indeed we do – we must not forget that variety is one of its ingredients, and it is no use to go on criticizing the Mediterranean for the patchwork system of its corporate life. (It remains to be seen, of course, when we have really got bureaucracy going, how long we can remain corporate ourselves.) However this may be, the Greco-Roman world, which still is the modern Mediterranean, discovered centuries ago that a body of regulations in the middle of one's path can only be dealt with by the most prompt and skilful circumvention. *'Fatta la legge, trovato l'inganno'* the Italians say: 'Make a law find a wa around it.

In this age-long struggle of the Individual against the Regulation, the government official, in whatever department it may be, is the adversary. But he is not therefore either black to your white, or white to your black, as he would be in our ethical North. He is a human being like ourselves, who has chosen to make his career in the camp opposed to human nature but retains the freedom as well as the power to be either

easy or disagreeable to his friends. There are any number of hidden little
bridges between the two Mediterranean camps. Nor is their intercourse
quite as unknown as we like to imagine it in the North. During the war,
I twice had to cross into and out of England without time to have all
my papers censored. The censor's rules were very strict and I had a
great many papers, collected for a tour on which I was being sent to the
U.S.A. I handed these in at the ports of arrival and departure, explaining
why they were not sealed and stamped as they should have been, and on
both occasions happened by great good fortune on an officer who knew
my books and took it upon himself to think it safe to let me have my
packet back unread. He too was using his individual judgement against
the regulations; and the fact that one sort of official will use it for the
general good and another for his own particular, is just one of those
human problems which hamper the regulations all the time.

I must digress to another pleasant breach which happened in 1938
when the democratic nations imposed the blockade called 'sanctions'
on Mussolini at the beginning of the Abyssinian war. My mother at that
time sent me from Italy to England a small strip of embroidery linen
which I needed. The little sample lingered on its way, but a large sheet
of paper reached me with full description of the policy of sanctions and
consequent detention of my parcel by His Majesty's Customs: and I was
so annoyed that I wrote back, explaining that I detested dictatorships
in general, and Mussolini's in particular, but could not see how my
embroidery linen could help while the tankers carrying oil were all
allowed freely through. Some unknown official evidently felt the same,
for the next post brought my parcel.

On looking back along the vista of my long and varied warfare with
the Customs, I am surprised to notice how many stimulating memories
these meetings contain. Even the French, who are apt to enjoy being
disagreeable as soon as they wear a uniform, have given me pleasurable
moments. There was a man on the *wagon-lits* who solved the problem of
a new Paris suit: one could get fourteen per cent, as far as I remember,
off its not inconsiderable price if one presented the parcel sealed and
intact at the exit from France, and one could avoid the Italian duty on
it if it lay, innocent and unwrapped from its tissue papers, among one's

ordinary clothes: one had just the time taken by the tunnel between the two countries to operate the transformation, and the attendant (who kept all the parcels in his cubby hole on the train) told me he was in the habit of doing this *'pour toutes les dames'*. In the middle of the night, as soon as the French Customs had been pacified, he handed in my parcel from the corridor, and a hasty unpacking and re-packing spread the cartons and name of Mme Gres into the darkness between Brigue and Domodossola.

Another friendly helper appeared at the beginning of the war when I was sent to Aden and was trying to get into the Orient Express in Paris with far more luggage than they allowed.

'I have eight frontiers to cross,' I explained; 'and my luggage is full of things I don't want them to see.'

'Let it go in,' said the guard, looking fiercely at the shrinking passengers inside. 'I too have worked for the Intelligence Service.' (I may say that my suitcases mostly contained innocuous and indeed futile propaganda films – such as 'Sheep-shearing in Yorkshire' or 'Arts and Crafts in England Today'.)

Recollections of unkind Customs officers are almost as agreeable as the others; they gave the pleasure of warfare without its serious pain.

There was a Frenchman on the Menton frontier whom I begged to let me and my car through quickly since my battery had given out and I was afraid, being a bad driver, to twist about in darkness on the Corniche road. He replied by going through every detail of my luggage with sadistic slowness, while I searched in a spasm of hatred for the most wounding thing I could find to say. The war was just over and feeling among the French ran high. 'He is surely a *collaborateur*.' I thought, and, drawing a bow at a venture: 'One can see, Monsieur, that you never fought at Bir Hakim,' I said. Bir Hakim was the desert site where the Free French covered themselves with glory, and the mention of it must have touched some delicate and unsuspected chord. The wicked man leaped into the air as if I had run a needle into him.

'What makes you say that, Mademoiselle?'

'That, Monsieur,' said I, noticing my advantage, 'is a matter I mean to keep to myself.'

I was luckily as innocent of contraband as could be, and when at last the darkness was falling and my luggage had to be closed: 'One says that the English are phlegmatic: I have never found them so', was my Frenchman's still furious comment.

'I presume no one has told you that women are phlegmatic?' was my retort. After which, as we were south of the Alps, he came round the barrier of the Customs and shook hands.

*   *   *   *   *

Some years ago I was discussing the question of the Persian nomads with one of the Bakhtiari Khans in Isfahan. These tribes move twice a year, up to their summer or down to their winter pastures, and are a menace to the quiet farmers on their way. 'We leave our villages and close our gates,' my Persian Mirza told me long before, 'when the tribes are passing by.'

'In a few years,' said the Bakhtiari (dressed in the best Scotch tweed and sipping his whisky), 'we shall have no more nomads: they will be settled peacefully on their lands.'

I took up what is a lost cause, since the process has already gone too far to stop; but I asked him whether the way of life that produces a maximum of independence, intelligence, toughness and self-reliance, is not perhaps worth trying to preserve at almost any cost in the empty and barren stretches of earth?

The same argument, I think, holds in favour of smuggling.

Our chief enemy today is neither Russia nor Africa nor China, but mere boredom in a world in which the means of living may be ceasing to be totally absorbing. Even animals suffer from this monster as soon as they enjoy security, as anyone can see who has not taken his dog out for a walk. It threatens, unless carefully neutralized, to play havoc in a world under control.

Crime begins to appear as the alternative to war.

Efforts are already being made to supply other and less damaging equivalents. Adventure – organized to be innocuous, or dangerous so as to be advertised; philanthropy – an almost boundless interference of efficient and inefficient people in other people's lives; even the pleasures of the imagination – as a last resort – are being enlisted. They all lack one or both of two indispensable ingredients: their appeal is either too narrow to be general, or the stimulus of danger is wanting.

The art of smuggling has these requisites in a manageable form. It should not be despised. It is less expensive than war and unlike crime does no real harm to innocent people; it merely robs a government already usually engaged in robbing, and in any case produces no such sensible loss as to outbalance its individual enjoyment. It encourages initiative and, like mountaineering or sailing (which often enter into its curriculum), has a spice of danger of its own: and adds, moreover, the animating sensation of stepping temporarily outside the bureaucratic bonds. In this it may perhaps in its small way be compared with what the cosmonauts feel when they slide outside their satellites in space.

I have never, as far as I remember, heard of anything either very cruel or vicious in the annals of smuggling, at any rate as practised today. The worst I can remember were two carabiniers tied back to back by the outlaws in the mountains and left for their comrades of the next patrol to find: or the frontier guards of Mussolini shooting at embarrassed climbers when some caprice of an Alpine ridge forced them up the wrong side of the border.

Usually it is clear fun, not too expensive to either side. In the Persian summer, when the embassies go camping up the valley of the Lar, the Military Secretary had been looking forward to the use of his new fishing-rod from London. The weeks went by and it lay in the Customs, marooned as if for ever; and when the last day before his holiday came round, his servant volunteered to steal it out. With the help of some useful oriental friend it was extracted from its package in the Customs' store, was used – no doubt with additional pleasure – by the Military Secretary, and replaced in unobserved safety when the holiday was over, to emerge and pay its duty in its official time.

On the borders of Egypt the camel caravans were used for the transport of hashish: the camels were fed with it, in pellets wrapped in some substance too hard to digest, which they were carefully timed to evacuate intact on the right (or wrong) side of the frontier.

I have never myself carried a narcotic of any kind and when I found a few packets of opium hidden in my saddle-bags by a Persian guide,

I risked the mutiny of my small caravan by throwing them in sight of all into a stream: the drug traffic is not amusing. It brings a dark note into the map of this otherwise cheerful game, and justifies the official contention that human nature is not to be trusted. If this were not so, if the individual used his judgement only to smuggle happiness and enjoyment across the borders of the world, and to leave things like hashish and gelignite alone, the official position would indeed be untenable and frontiers even more idiotic than they are.

Even as it is there is a fallacy inherent in the effort to substitute law for human nature which – as I have been trying to show – will inevitably appear, however much you dress it up in uniform. 'Dress them as you like; they will always run away', the King of Naples is reported to have said of his poor soldiers; and the only remedy is not to be found in the regulations as such at all but lurks in whatever reality there may exist behind a legal façade.

The persuasive strength of truth is in the long run the only substitute for crime, from the illegal smoking of a cigarette to the exploding of an atomic bomb: it is only through the conscience of mankind that these questions can be touched. I am not suggesting that this can be achieved, since Christianity and other religions also have tried for about two thousand years and failed: but the difficulty of a path in the right direction does not make the easier and the wrong one any the more likely to lead to one's goal: and the probability is that humanity in general will continue to think that a woman in Italy has as much claim to a whiff of French perfume as a woman in Paris. While this conviction persists in spite of economic laws, smuggling is most likely to continue; and as it offers one of the few harmless sports that can in any way be comparable with war it is quite a good idea to make use of our silly frontiers while we have them, and let our youth be trained, as the Spartans trained theirs, by stealing. We are in a poor way perhaps, and if we are reduced to seeing our good wheat stifled (largely by bureaucratic regulations), we may as well do what we can to extract some living virtue from the tares.

1966

These last essays are tinged with a natural sadness, because they have been written in the catastrophe of an empire in whose hopes and dreams I too had my passionate share. One may look back and see how the miracle was not the empire's end but its actual existence – for our island in the North Sea is very small; or one may look forward to geographic causes, shiftings of trade routes to and from ancient bases, things that have been and will be, carrying the lives of men and nations in their wake: there are other hopes and other dreams, and no spring will come without a new carpet of flowers over the graves of a generation that fought its two long wars: they are fitted into the roots of our being, too deep for oblivion, in the permanent sub-structure of our world.

Time

Even such is time, which takes in trust
Our youth, our joys, our all we have,
And pays us but with age and dust.
Who in the dark and silent grave,
When we have wandered all our ways,
Shuts up the story of our days. . . .[1]

There is no active malignity, no bitterness of hatred or warmth of affection, no wish to devour, in Time. Himself inert, and in fact non-existent, he is the sea in which men grow, are born, or die; and apart from his indifferent monotony, nothing in him is fixed to stand – no death, no splendour, no apotheosis, no end in sight – nothing but a neutral field for revolution. The world's picture of him, active to seal up and to destroy, the picture of Chronos eating his children, is imaginative but not true.

In tapestries and allegorical pictures, nereids, tritons, sea-horses, dolphins roll and play in a dark blue ocean which has always appeared to me as the sea of Time. They emerge (usually half-way) and disappear, and it is unfair to blame that horizon-bounded playground for their disappearance. They have the sun and sky to watch them and the sea-rim for the arena of their world, and it is up to them not to mourn for the fact that the playtime is limited, but to remember rather that for a short and brilliant interval the enlivening of that particular flatness of water rests in their hands alone. Their business, as I have just said, is revolution.

I like to contemplate revolution as a something the tritons undertake for fun. It is surely a natural, but a mistaken, idea to think of it in more sombre terms, a perversion of an everyday occurrence, much as if one were to consider eating only in terms of indigestion. To anyone who keeps his mind alive, revolution has the ease of a natural function, a briskness inherent in human nature, which without it would still be chipping flints (if indeed it had got so far). It is the mind's equivalent to the body's breathing, and ideas fresh or faded should be as smooth in their coming and going as the physical air that empties and fills our lungs. It should in fact be a pleasant operation, and it is only because we have fallen into the habit of contemplating its grim side only that our attitude to revolution has come to be unfriendly.

There is a spring day when the fire feels too hot and doors are opened, and we decide to have our first meal out of doors: a small bustling takes place with tablecloths and glasses and the life of the household is adapted to the spring. It is revolution in miniature, but it is genuine revolution – an adaptation for the better for all concerned. If the housewife is recalcitrant, the thing becomes embittered and may fail; if the family choose a bad day and the winter returns to pounce on them, the whole thing will have to be given up and started again later; and if granny suffers from bronchitis and cannot take the air, she will have to be wrapped in shawls or found a sheltered corner, or arranged in separate comfort altogether – for one should not have revolutions, domestic or otherwise, that lop off from us the human bits that are, after all, our own.

With these provisos, revolution is man's normal activity, and if he is wise he will grade it slowly so that it may be almost imperceptible – otherwise it will jerk in fits and starts and cause discomfort: but its game will ever be that of the dolphins and tritons, emerging and disappearing in their sea of Time. And when he thinks it out, the revolutionary is rather surprised to discover that the main necessity on both sides of a revolution is *kindness*, which makes possible the most surprising things. To treat one's neighbour as oneself is the fundamental maxim for revolution.

1966

On Silence

The Arabs, both the bedouin in their tents and city folk as I knew them, cultivate an interval of silence in their talk. After the hot summer day in Baghdad, when one's lipstick had melted and one's heels had sunk into the asphalt pavements, and fans had revolved slowly all day in rooms sealed at every opening against the heat, one would join a circle in some starlit garden and drink the bitter, delicious coffee of the desert or the sticky Turkish kind, or tea in slim glasses decorated with blue and red spots and gaudy lettering; and the evening would slip by until eleven or midnight, when a substantial dinner was carried out on trays, and one would eat and with no further loitering go home. In this easy intercourse there was excellent conversation, for the Arabs in their centuries of leisure (enhanced by a frequent absence of lamplight) have ever been good raconteurs, and their manners are perfect: I have never known them to interrupt, or to speak too loud, or to break away into a private talk during a general conversation. But when they had nothing particular to say, there was silence, and no one thought anything of it.

To the newcomer from the West there was at first a feeling of embarrassment in a circle of ten or twelve people sitting – for five or six minutes perhaps – absolutely dumb: women in particular would rush into the breach and fill it more or less promiscuously with words. But very soon the comfort of not having to make conversation unless one had something to say became apparent, and one was in danger of becoming so happy in the Arab convention as to bring it back to the drawing-rooms of the West.

One would not, of course, think of the Arab pauses as silence absolute, but they were anterooms of silence, as it were, and a recognition of its existence, even in the midst of conversation.

Silence is, as a matter of fact, a stranger in our world, known only by her absence. No human being, I suppose, has ever met the perfect stillness, though we can imagine and indeed love it, think of it as subtly connected with our most intimate moments of rapture, and feel certain that there is no perfect bliss without it. The heavens are mute when the angels sing, and Dante, in his Paradise, describes the lark as rising into a voiceless beatitude that at last satisfies her heart.

Dante no doubt heard the celestial singing, but our human larks are tied to the hum of a world in which their nest lies visible below. Even in the desert, where there is only sand, and the wind meets nothing that can give it a voice, there is always a faint ethereal piping and the sound of the slipping of innumerable particles into infinitesimal hollows – a feeble rustling that one could imagine in moments of depression to be the plaintive but busy murmur of humanity in the ear of a distant God.

The sea, of course, is never silent. I have often thought that if our ear were finer, it would catch the soft, smooth friction between the glassy wave top and the resisting air. Even far out, when a still day lies like metal on the oily surface, and the lazy patches of the sun dilate between imperceptible rises, a little wave will suddenly raise its head out of nothingness with a plop and subside into nothingness again: and yet when those days have fulfilled us with their long, empty hours, and in spite of the interrupted but fairly continuous rap of canvas against a mast, the feeling we take home is that of silence, the thing we have never known.

The moon is said to be quite quiet, and, now that her landscape is becoming fashionable, our astronauts may yet make the acquaintance of the veiled figure that moves beyond the substance of our earth. Long ago up there a sizzling boiling noise must have existed, as it still does with us in places – by the island of Santorin, for instance, which is the southernmost of the Greek islands before you reach the Cretan sea; it has little left except the few remaining teeth of a volcano, decayed and irregular, around a crater bay too deep for ships to anchor; and the townlets, sunning themselves along the top of this denture, get the amenities of their life from gentler slopes that fan out with fields and vineyards from the precipice circle, outward towards the open sea. In 1925 the eyes of the citizens were riveted on the depths of their bay below, where a small subsidiary island was suddenly appearing. It is there now – an ugly, mineral, shapeless mass, and one can still cook an egg, they told me, in its cindery crevices; its small crepitations and sterile landslides are the only noises of a life that in time will no doubt resemble that of the rest of our world today. Of course it is comforting, in a way, to look down from the whitewashed Santorin houses and observe that in spite of our misdeeds and misgivings the world we live in is more attractive now than when it was first made.

Polar explorers come to know as much of terrestrial silence as anyone can. For my part, I have been nearest to it among mountains. Sounds are mere accidents in those recesses – detachment of rocky fragments, avalanches, the drip of melting glaciers, the rumble of thunder coiling in snaky defiles, the sinister falling of stones: the mountain self is immune, and what one listens to is not the sound but its fading into the unlimited repose that wraps and folds it like a garment, as if the mountain mother were soothing the infant earth in its cradle below. It is nearly always this rounding into stillness that the mountain poets remember – even Coleridge, battling with Mont Blanc in the darkness and 'visited all night by troops of stars'.

I once climbed Monte Rosa by the Marinelli *couloir*[1]. We walked up to the hut for seven hours from the Italian side at Macugnaga, and there had to wait for the midnight cold to freeze the avalanche ice above; we could then cross the *couloir* – a half-hour or so of horizontal stepcutting – in comparative safety, and proceed up the steep glacier as if climbing the precipitous side of a wave. Having reached the hut early, I spent the afternoon hours on a small, safe ledge nearby, watching the avalanches as they hurtled down below me – every ten or fifteen minutes, as I remember. The *couloir* lay – white and polished ice, broad as the Nile but giddily tilted – and the snows of the great wavelike mountain frothed down it like milk in a churn; the soft, threatening hiss of their tossing reached me as they poured swiftly below and were lost in the roar of their descent; I still remember how this reverberation fell over some precipice, and how the silence wrapped it, as if the armies of the world had been engulfed.

Another recollection of this sound-silence symphony stays with me vividly from my mountaineering days, and that is the rustle of the broken ice as it slides from the ice-cutter's pickaxe above one: one's own axe is sharply pointed into the smooth slope to hold in case of a slip, and one has time, however precariously, to look about while that busy, mouselike rustle of sharp fragments seethes round one's big boots on its way into darkness below. As we climbed in and out of the *sèracs*, the broken ice cliffs, that overhang Macugnaga, the valley and the whole world, as it seemed in our moonlight, lay azure in sleep and shadow. Here the mountain is almost vertical, and we could rest by leaning slightly against it without bending, while our guide halted us among the juttings of ice to listen for the smallest crackle of sound that might spell danger: the silence is the mountain's peace.

But the best silence is on the summit, when one has achieved it and is resting on whatever space there may be: and that, too, is no silence, but a compound of all voices that rise from earth and lose themselves in air. Sometimes one can just hear them separately – if the peak is not too high, and the day is clear: one can hear the faint murmur of torrents interrupted by the breezes that bear their voices, and shut or release them as with the fanning of a hand, as I have heard the mutter of rapids on a bend of the Euphrates far below. But mostly, on a fine day, it is a hymn of space and sunlight in which sound has become visual and is not heard but seen. It is the lark's view, and her nest is somewhere in it; and the human heart recognizes itself as a living note in something that is neither sight nor sound, nor notes nor music, but an offering on the altar of all the world in sight. I have often been asked what is the joy of mountaineering, and I think that perhaps it is this communion, the consummation of one's own toil and danger, the answer that life makes to death.

For it must be remembered that silence can be dead or living, and the two kinds must be distinguished. And perhaps the poles of Being are in the distinction – the one an end and a downfall and a destruction, and the other a part of that which has neither beginning nor end: and even in the humblest instance there is a difference in the silence of these two.

There is, for instance, regrettably often a noticeable blank in the wedded silence, when a couple have been married for some time. One sees them in restaurants or on cruises – middle-aged, averted faces that turn towards each other with no light in their eyes and drop words of such astonishing triviality that one wonders how the air consents to carry them: surely the sort of conversation Sartre was thinking of when he described Hell as one prolonged domestic scene.

Yet if a young creature were to ask for advice whether to say yes or no to the manor woman she or he thought of marrying, one might do worse than to ask: 'Are you happy to be silent together?' That companionship is the living silence – a relaxation that finds speech superfluous, an atmosphere of well-being where nothing needs to be explained, a part of that current which can make not only men but most living things happy to be together. It is, I like to imagine, the stream that flows beneath all differences of race or of language and carries each one of us from those cindery beginnings towards our undiscovered end.

It is also valid between men and animals, and I have felt it with my horse when sharing a sandwich beside some sun-warmed granite boulder out of the wind during a day's idleness across the Dartmoor moors. It is wonderful in wild animals when their hearts are given to human beings: an Arabian lizard which I once spent two months in taming would relax in my hand when frightened and curl up in the safety of the familiar touch, and it was a constant wonder to me to find our feelings so similar – our pleasure in the warmth of the sun, our curiosities and playfulness (the little creature would toss its head for fun when tickled), and even the capacity for affection – every human warmth, in fact, racing through that cold blood.

*   *   *   *   *

A part of all art is to make silence speak. The things left out in painting, the note withheld in music, the void in architecture – all are as necessary and as active as the utterance itself. I have often thought of this in a cathedral, watching the Gothic spaces move into their shadows, or in the mosques of Istanbul, where I would slip my shoes off and turn in for a short rest when the cobbled streets left me exhausted. The so-called New Mosque, with its late but beautiful blue tiles, was near the terminus of my Bosphorus steamer, and I would sit there on my way and watch not the structure but the space it enclosed, in whose dimness the barefoot people touched their foreheads to the ground. In Saint Sophia this beauty of emptiness that has acquired a shape seems to me more visible than in any other building I know. These things, too, are voices of silence, which is as inseparable from any sort of utterance as a shadow from its sun.

In literature silence has to be expressed by various devices, of which punctuation is the most obvious and least adequate. There are subtler ways, and it might be profitable to a young writer to take up John Milton, for instance, and watch how he shepherds his readers, especially at the conclusion of his works, into the repose that is the written equivalent of silence. Just as his opening of *Paradise Lost* is like a trumpet call:

> Of that forbidden tree whose mortal taste
> Brought death into the world and all our woe. . .

so the end is a vague stillness that lets time and eternity and the quiet pacing of the universe wrap the reader's mind and draw it from its tumult through a pacified estuary to its sea:

> The world was all before them, where to choose
> Their place of rest, and Providence their guide:
> They hand in hand, with wand'ring steps and slow,
> Through Eden took their solitary way.

The westering sun in *Lycidas* has 'stretched out all the hills'; the end of *Samson Agonistes*, 'all passion spent', is at one with the concluding gentleness of *Paradise Regained*.

The device is apparent in all Milton's longer poems: the subtle cadences leave us soothed in a final reconcilement:

> He, unobserv'd,
> Home to His Mother's house private return'd.

His endings all sink into this waveless peace.

The great poets play thus with their silence, Matthew Arnold, in the description of the River Oxus – the most beautiful of all his descriptions, to my mind – varies the movement and the stillness, the tumult and its cessation, from the beginning of this little jewel to its end. The 'hushed Chorasmian waste' comes as near as any sound can to the essence of quiet; and after the bright speed of Oxus 'in his high mountain-cradle of Pamere',

> His luminous home of waters opens, bright
> And tranquil, from whose floor the new bathed stars
> Emerge, and shine upon the Aral sea.

No image of noise can intrude upon this majesty.

There is no great regard for quietness in our world today. Apart from the mixed motives with which journeys to the moon are being facilitated, the pursuit of silence as such has gone out of fashion, together with sunrises, autumn walks through fading woodlands, the enjoyment – which few people relish – of the passing of time, and all these delicately sentimental pleasures that belonged to the Romantic Age. When I was young, one could still say that one had got up early for the sun, but it would be a very remote place where such an activity would not be thought eccentric now.

I could perhaps still find one or two such oases.

In 1956 I happened to be at a local festival held in an ancient townlet called Erdek, west of Istanbul on the Sea of Marmara's southern shore. I believe it has now become popular and developed, but at that time the festival was scarcely known, except to a small society of Turkish intellectuals who came to act a few excellent plays on a stage rigged in a pine wood, and to recite each other's poems with some very long introductions in prose. The country people gathered, sat in long rows on their sea walls or drank lemonade and coffee in the open, watching their festival with a happy boredom, as a mother might the uninteresting games of her child, which are yet in a way a product of herself. My friends had found me a clean, scrubbed and hand-embroidered room in the cottage of two old Bulgarian refugees, and our four days passed in a tumultuous leisure made pleasant by the sea. Little motor-boats under cotton awnings would take us for a *lira* or so to one of the sandy beaches, and it was only when evening was falling and the cafés grew more crowded that its natural quiet returned to the bay of Erdek's grass-grown old acropolis.

Strolling back from a walk at this hour, I fell in with one of the inhabitants, who also seemed a little lost in the four-day rhapsody of his town.

'What do you do to amuse yourselves all the rest of the year?' I asked him.

We were standing where the coarse grass meets the sand, and the sun was sinking, with its light laid on the bay like the straightness of a sword.

'When there Is no festival?' said he. 'We come to this place each evening from our houses to see the sunset.'

The Romantic Age evidently still existed in Erdek.

It has probably gone now, and anyway the citadel of silence is being breached in all directions. In the Alps, though I am no skier, I love to be taken in winter by one of the open ski-lifts over the pathless snow; that is silence as near as we can get it, a trancelike dream under one's dangling feet. One could mount up from Cortina in three stages, and at last, at an altitude of about 7,000 feet, see the whole of the Dolomite ranges bathed in their winter radiance, not white but pale sun-on-snow, as if it were the straw-coloured halo of a saint. The skiers whizzed over a sunny shoulder, but the ski-lift mounted straight and steep through shadow on the far side, with not a sound except for the thud of a snow load from the lower trees and the moan of the machinery as one's chair negotiated a tower. Below it the mountain slope lay white and soft as a sea-bird's breast, until one stepped into the normal world of the hut among one's fellows at the top. This pleasure is now wrecked by the fact that the Italians have provided their ski-lift towers with loudspeakers, so that even the short transit from Cortina to the upper snows may be done to the sound of jazz.

In a Hans Christian Andersen tale the nightingale is ousted by its mechanical counterpart, yet its singing – too rarefied for the courtiers' ears – comforts the emperor's solitary sickbed in the night. With us, too, the real music, imagined yet never actually heard, grows increasingly difficult to discover; yet many, even among those who are unaware of being dissatisfied with a world of noise, will still open their hearts if they happen unawares upon the undertones of silence.

I will bring one more instance from the unsophisticated backwaters of Turkey, where the loudspeaker is now turned on for you whenever you enter any shabby little bar. This happened to a party of us about half-way down the western coast of Asia Minor (the gulf that pushes east from Bodrum, the Halicarnassus of the ancients). It hits a precipice of Anatolia, little frequented either by boats or by cars. A shallow, reedy inlet is crossed by a bridge of wooden palings blistered by many seasons of salt and sun; and long strings of camels still pass along it in the morning or evening light. A Lycian tomb or two, on carved pillars, is cut into the amphitheatre of the cliff, and the only other building visible was a new house with an inappropriate bar attached to it, just above the lapping of the waves on their shingle.

The barman's jazz seemed to splinter the golden afternoon. I declared it unbearable: but my eldest godson, who is far kinder than I am, said it would be ungentle to hurt the feelings of the barman, so proud of his new toy. 'It must be done, and I shall try,' said I, and began by telling the man how beautiful we found his secluded land: ' . . . and how lucky you are,' I went on, 'to be living here where the waves come to your doorstep as quiet and gay as music. Would you mind turning off your wireless, so that we can listen to their little whispers on your beach?'

The man had obviously never noticed his waves before, but he understood that he had something better than his wireless to offer, and was pleased.

Such is silence: a creature never met in this world and present only through sound, her opposite and her earthly companion. Her own true shape we cannot know, and if ever she steps among us with her noiseless feet, we listen entranced to the gentlest echoes of our world and time, that tell us she is there. Out of pure faith we believe in her unproved existence, and it needs only one further step to convince us that beyond her the silence of the mystics exists also, in a serenity in which life itself is but a flash and an interruption: in which those very words that have been our solace and delight are no longer needed; and all barriers are down.

1966

Our Second-rate Security

If I have a free morning in London, I sometimes find my way to the zoo. There, in the reptile house, I once saw some snakes and lizards boxed, strangely enough, together, in a glass case with rocks and small cacti round them. The thin brown snakes slid or poured like water down their miniature hollows; the lizards, fixing a lidless look of class-conscious vacuity on space, sat panting with double chins and taut tummies against the warmth of rock. How strange, I thought, to see the feeders and the fed like this together; and wondered if my conception of a serpent's diet might be wrong. Snakes might be vegetarian after all.

At this moment one coil, polished like brown leather and actually supporting a drowsy lizard in its bend, suddenly contracted; the head of the unsuspecting guest was held between two triangles of fang; the huge mouthful was progressing almost imperceptibly and quite passively out of sight into the throat (if that is what a snake has) and I watched fascinated while first the shoulders and next the two arms disappeared. I looked round for any sign of emotion among the other lizards: no flicker of fear or pity showed; it might have been Tibet for all they cared. So much for Security, I thought.

Lizards in a cage can do little about their destiny, but most animals take precautions, especially when they eat. Even a cat or dog, if it happens to be something that he likes, will carry his tit-bit to a corner and turn his back, as if his friends had suddenly become unsafe. Small birds will look at their food from every angle before they pounce. In Barbados they would fly in and out of my room as if it were their territory, and would chase any intruder away with a chatter of protest and bristling wings. They would come so near as to perch on the handle of my cup while I held it, and though I never could induce them to drink, they would take my bread, broken in small pieces, and morning after morning would post themselves at strategic angles, to see if there could be any possible ambush before they fluttered down and carried it away; nor did they ever feel it safe to snatch this little bite on trust. Their carefulness no doubt gave them a feeling of minor safety in a dangerous world, such as we have when we put on a seat-belt in a car.

It matters little whether the human race is more like the lizards in their cage or like those others that are free to organize their illusions: the problem of safety essential to human happiness goes far beyond both animal boundaries. It is more complex than such basic wants as hunger, love, or fear, that hit with a recognizable and reasonable impulse — accepted or rejected, one usually makes no mistake as to their identity. But security, our habitable climate, is pursued through all disguises, a will-'o-the-wisp down every variety of by-path to the outposts of the world; and beckons to us beyond them; and because it seems so unattainable and is so vital, we play with it although it is not there, and dress ourselves in a safety which we might as well call non-existent, since it is helpless where its validity is most required, against vicissitude and time.

'There are no wars any longer', says Epictetus the slave: 'nor battles, no brigandage on a large scale, nor piracy — at any hour we may travel by land, or sail from the rising of the sun to its setting. Can Caesar then at all provide us with peace from fever too, and from shipwreck and fire or earthquake or lightning? Come, can he give us peace from love?'

Anything less than this peace is subsidiary, a trickle doomed to be swamped sooner or later in the quagmires of disaster or death. The ages of faith alone — almost any faith — have been able to stride through and scatter their immortal ruins over landscapes less comfortable than ours. They achieved this by adding a dimension to their ordinary lives, and so organized their security within the wider frame.

Whatever our faith or lack of faith may be, this *wider frame* must be sought, comprehensive enough for something better than a second-rate safety within the prison bounds. Many people, humble or exalted too, possess it, though the ages of faith are in abeyance. A friend of mine, riding along the Sudan frontier, told me how his barefoot guide had trodden on one of the horned vipers coloured like the desert, whose bite is mortal. Brandy was brought and they urged him to drink it as medicine. 'It will save you,' they told him. But the old Muslim put it gently away. 'I am too near paradise to drink brandy,' he said; and wrapped himself in his white woollen cape, and lay on the ground to die; the frame of his own security in its desert barrier was sufficient.

A similar but less final experience came to me and my two godsons in Turkey as we were crossing the Taurus and our guide fell ill. I too gave him brandy and told him it was medicine, and although he had seemed at death's door the taste of it made him leap up and cry that I had given him what was forbidden, and look as if he meant to kill us (for he was extremely ready with his gun). I reflected that he must have tasted the medicine at least once to recognize it, but kept this to myself and managed to pacify him, and decided never again to risk a man's convictions for the less important saving of his life.

This, if we come to think of it, is exactly what the social safety of our day is doing. It is Martha, trying to get the upper hand; and whatever her success, however comfortable she makes us, however splendid her philanthropy or rich her science, it will ever be fatal to forget for a single moment that her security is nil. This is the rock on which kingdoms have toppled and nations will topple again: and the only way, as far as I can see, to overstep it is to look steadily at the background of our insurances, our discoveries, our furniture as it were, and see their sun and shadow, their good and evil, entire – their grief and pain not huddled to a corner but given a meed of honour, humanity's sombre temporal crown; for there is no safety like accepted danger. On no account should children be too much sheltered from the nobility of this severe regard any more than from the blustering winter weathers: and this more than ever now that we live so much in towns where the natural shadows of our panorama are apt to be distorted, and the country no longer anchors our true safety by making us familiar with our fears.

I can remember, without any particular strengthening of philosophy, the peculiar taste of the acceptance of death. I was climbing with a friend in the Rosengarten, and we took a guide for the Vaiolet tower, smooth but creased like an elephant's skin and sheer in its mineral beauty, nearly vertical from a stony valley. About half-way up my companion, helped by the guide, went out of sight to reach a jag where the rope was wound, while I, the last on the line, waited to follow. The rope has to be exceptionally long on these Dolomite towers, as the belaying places are few and far apart; it hung suspended, limp and solitary – a lifeline between the little crack where my friends had disappeared and my waist, where I stood on a small ledge; and from there, when I heard the shout above, I prepared to follow. I had nearly reached the crack when my boot slipped from the tiny crease that is here the only foothold, and I dropped into space: the rope held, with an unpleasant jerk round my ribs, and finding itself in the character of a pendulum with a living weight attached, swung slowly out round the bastion of the tower, far, far above the valley and its mountain pastures and white and stony streams. I travelled gently, and had leisure to notice the wrinkled texture of the wall I was almost touching, and the bowl of the landscape with its radiating watersheds far below. I felt a slight nausea as I saw my hat revolving in the sunny air on its way down through space, and, into a feeling of panic that was invading me, death suddenly took its place to my surprise; I felt that nothing worse could happen, and that I could take it; and the clutch of fear left as if it were a knot being untied. When the rope swung its pendulum back again I knew I must seize my chance; I clamped myself to my ledge and scrambled successfully this time, and found my party peacefully unaware, though my friend asked if I were tired, as I looked pale. On our way down in the late afternoon, as we strode easily through the snowy patches and damp pastures, with the rope untied and the whole circle of the Rosengarten glowing behind us, I told them what had occurred. The mountain happiness, cool and pure as its waters, was all around us, and the morning's climb was already half lost in shadow; Vaiolet lifted her small flat summit like an altar under the hammer strokes of the ages into the evening light; and there, it seemed to me, I could see death and life inseparably welded, as I had discovered them – it gave me a strange exultation – that very morning in myself.

The world too, at this moment, looks as if it were suspended against a mountain wall where it must either drop or climb, for never has it been more hideously insecure; and death is not as menacing or alien as the black cruelty that lies, nearer to us than ever before, a dragon asleep in all our peaceful lands. What safety can we talk of when at any instant it may wake? If we could really think that social works can save us, how would we differ from those lizards in their cage?

> All things invite
> To peaceful counsels and the settled state
> Of order, how in safety best we may
> Compose our present evils, with regard
> Of what we are and where, dismissing quite
> All thoughts of war.[1]

It is the security which Milton lets Mammon describe in Hell. And the structure of science is but a blister in the wastelands of Babel when the yardstick is infinity – misleading if it leads us to forget that its limit is the boundary of our prison and not a step beyond. For our problem is that of Archimedes, and the lever by which our universe is to be lifted must be founded on something more basic than the universe itself.

If this essay were being written for the believer, the matter could here be left in the arms of faith. But I write for the doubtful: a nomad in the suburbs of civilization, I pick out of its unregarded heaps such untheologic facts as I can find and turn them over, and look at them with wonder, and try to understand – this heavy sodden mess, for instance, of sorrow and of pain.

It has no dragon blackness, it is not evil; it is a part, like rocks and fire, of the hardness of the world. Yet no God can share it, no divinity can touch without dissolving it: while it exists, it is the sad prerogative of man. The Christian God abdicates to enter the precincts of pain; they are man's exclusively, and the virtues that belong to them are man's virtues – fortitude, pity, patience, endurance – engrained in the roughness of Time, they are meaningless beyond. Milton has not denied them to Lucifer in his exile; they inhabit the well-appointed town in the first book of *Paradise Lost* which has so definitely modern a planning touch about it, with only the heavenly horizon and the presence of God denied.

These things the poet and the saint have seen, and even to our average sight the horizon is given. But whatever the abyss from which it comes, the darkness of pain is here in our sunniest landscape, a blot no government can tackle or science dispel. Our frame of security must find room for sorrow, together with cruelty and death; and no welfare state can do more than make us tolerably comfortable while things go tolerably well.

Yet in beauty unimaginable, beauty in every opening leaf untouched by fear, we would never look beyond the radiance of our world if sorrow were not its inhabitant. The angels might be about us, and we would not see them: we would be in prison and not know it; and whatever Divinity there is would walk in His garden alone. Nothing but the transitory will make man look for the eternal, nor will he ever accept the one as substitute for the other, for such is the innate nobility of man. His human dignity, his attribute of pain, his crown of thorns is no bridge across chaos: but nothing else can make him look to see if a bridge is there. This precious incentive he will not consent to lose, whatever the cost may be. And let Martha by all means look to our earthly comfort, for we need it badly; but let her not call it security.

1967

Decadence, or The Bed of Procrustes

After a long interval, I have again read Cyril Connolly's *The Unquiet Grave*, and found in it the feeling of well-being and intimacy I remembered, which sincerity in literature can give.

How disillusioned is the opening sentence, read in my later light! 'The true function of a writer is to produce a masterpiece and no other task is of any consequence,' and few – he continues – having admitted this conclusion, 'will be prepared to lay aside the piece of iridescent mediocrity on which they have embarked.'

I pondered this sentence, thinking of the author himself, and of those among the writers I have known who also did not follow mediocrity and had it in them to reach a masterpiece up its steep path – Max Beerbohm in the past that seems so much farther than it is, John Sparrow in the ivory Shalott of All Souls: many more no doubt, but these actually accomplished mastery and in all three it could have been or could be much more. Something failed, not in them, since the seed of perfection was in them, but in the climate of their time: the 'iridescent mediocrity' perhaps, whose paralyzing hood I, with no thought of masterpiece, still look at with the eyes of a mouse in front of a cobra. I proceeded to follow its expanding authority in my imagination, from first awakening to literature in childhood when mediocrity was unsuspected and the classics were all about us, and Lamb's *Tales from Shakespeare* were forbidden till we could 'read a great poet in himself'; until through the tangles of our wars I reached our decadence today.

We may as well say the word.

Twenty-two years ago in England we touched the summit of prestige and power; the descent has been so swift that the Greece of Pericles, and after, is the only parallel that comes to mind. The measure of our bankruptcy is such that we hesitate to admit it to ourselves.

The victory we knew is lost even to her very features: the shipwreck she prevented is ousted from history, since it never happened; it is naturally forgotten, and we fought and won and came home with listless and strangely tired hearts to wipe up the mess and watch our victory's gilt fade from her laurels. We set up the Welfare State and the Festival of Britain, and put primroses on our postage stamps to show ourselves 'merely rural' (as the curate said of Mont Blanc): but none of these things have succeeded in giving us back the happy confidence of youth. The decadence is there, and anyone can spot it, from a lack of candour in public life to the fact that scarce a clock in any London street now tells the time correctly – from right and left in chaos to eccentricities of dress.

Many of these symptoms are straws that any wind might carry. Fashion in particular is always unreliable and a jack-in-the-box for the unexpected, bad or good. Petronius died like a gentleman though he dressed carefully, and heroism, welling like some fresh water from the world's basic darkness, has never been a matter of class. The noblest and the sorriest ages bear their children one like the other. What happens later, what forms and phenomena they deck themselves with, is like foam dissolving on waves that can by no means stabilize the sands of time they cover; their fluid arabesque need not detain us, but rather that hidden force beneath it, pushing it with sonorous monotony ashore. What power lifts it with such pulsation, such raising and lowering of nations, which we call progress and decay?

As far as one life can trace these movements, I seem to remember a parting of ways at the end of the first World War, a cleavage between my own generation – pre-1914 and practically wiped out – and those only a few years younger who took the pinchbeck of the Twenties for gold. The shock of 1914, after perhaps the longest general peace in history, caused a disturbance now nearly forgotten, for which no one was prepared. Our minds are hardened for war today for better or worse, but we then watched it out of the unknown, as Andromeda watched the dragon; and when the battle was over, the values of a whole generation lay spread about the rocks and turned to stone. In the perplexities that followed, two particular fallacies began or continued to spread, with a poison virulent enough, it seems to me, to explain decadence not only in literature but in every other mainspring of our life as well: they fostered mediocrity, the parent of decline.

Mediocrity, the level we tread on, the golden mean, the weft and woof of habit, the vine and fig-tree of Isaiah, the man in the street of today, framework of our world and honour of an age that tries to build happiness for all: under no circumstance should one question its modest and essential validity.

But it is another matter when this handmaid of our existence tries to wear the ornaments of Excellence, an essence separate not in degree (attainable by ordinary progression), but in kind (which requires a different approach). The fallacy that the one leads to the other is decadence itself: the river that delights even in shallow places can never lead again to its deep wells. A second fallacy followed close upon the first and still maintains itself: if the first-rate is out of reach, it advises, the second-rate will do.

Now excellence comes out of the deep well and is either reached by its own paths or not reached at all. It cannot be helped by being turned into something else and must either be itself or nothing. It is not a result, but an apparition. Its quality is to live out of reach and never to be attained – not even in the consciousness of those who attain it. It is whatever life may mean apart from daily living, a wisp of azure, a visitation to the mind or heart. Its genuine though only potential equality is insulted when any section of humanity is excluded from its aristocracy, general to religion and art and to many communities such as those of the desert people, whose intrinsic freedom is regardless of worldly accidents and all material things. It is probably because of this freedom that so many of us are happy among those whose winds blow as they list; but the happiness can be found, too, among craftsmen who delight in their plans, and ploughmen who drive a symmetric furrow, and anyone who is allowed for his daily enjoyment to dip into the timeless world where every perfection, small or great, is born.

This is that excellence where

> each in his separate star
> Shall draw the thing as he sees it
> For the God of things as they are:

where

> A man's reach must exceed his grasp,
> Or what's a heaven for?

It was obviously not unknown to Edwardians and Victorians and indeed can never become a stranger while a spark of the divine Outside illuminates this planet. A small inscription, written by a fine Turkish calligrapher a century ago, hangs in my house and tells, concisely, that 'this world is a seed-plot for the next': its smooth perfection within so small a compass, its obviously un-industrial carelessness of all except the target set up by itself for itself, still carry their atmosphere of harmony between the artist and his universe, a happiness humble but uncompromising.

This is excellence – the following of anything for its own sake and with its own integrity – and it is not to be served by any mere answer to a public demand. If the public becomes more important than the *maker*, artist, craftsman, labourer or even employee (whom no employer has the right to shut out from his own eternities) the seeds of decadence are sown and begin to flourish under their creeping economic laws: the creative side of life disappears, and decadence is sure.

This has, I think, happened since the First World War.

It is not that people were better before than after, for the human average does not seem to change and the start in the race is the same. People are not necessarily chaste when they believe in chastity, or brave when they believe in courage. But the target of the heroic age is set above its recognized possibilities, and the number of those who reach towards it is therefore increased; their eyes are lifted to the hills and their strength is augmented; what they dream is counted in their favour: on no account should we lower the standard of dreams.

After the 1914 deluge it became fashionable to do so; standard and conduct were to be identical, and like beggars – perhaps because we felt naked – we became determined to avoid hypocrisy and exhibit all our ulcers. Our disciplines had landed us in trouble and we rested on our oars in a victorious sunset while a whole generation looked round for relaxation. In all that deeply mattered, morality, religion, education, life or love, it was held for tolerance to esteem the second-rate as equal to the first – non-interference was the smug denomination.

A younger generation whom this gospel left unguarded has naturally revolted: the decadence was not in them but in their parents, where they have been spotting it with the merciless acumen of youth. It succeeded in proving that excellence was practically out of reach and no amount of mediocrity would coax it to be born; and our second fallacy, coming to terms with imperfection, soon showed itself to be even more fatal, since it shut away everything we truly live for, our door of vision in the passing world: there is scarcely a political speech or an advertisement in England today that does not fence the whole of life with material fences, averages offered as security or profit to the young. 'The hungry sheep look up and are not fed'; the hopeful sign is that they turn away.

It would be desperate to watch our hemisphere rolling into night without a certainty of dawn, and day will come, we may be sure: yet not so safely sure that our own people will carry its banner. Whatever symbol that is to be made of, heroism must go to its making, and heroism in war or peace, life or death, is a dedication to the unattainable and no product of mediocrity. The chances and the path through the dark are in the hands of the young.

With our setback behind us, we had better leave the future to them. Yet age can trace fragments of the past through their tangle, and it is peace and refreshment to oneself to get at some truth if one can. I would not like anything that I write in my evening leisure to be misleading either through hope or fear: and though I think I see the work of those two fallacies in almost everything we do, in business, love, and life, it would need a stronger voice than mine to make the danger clear across so wide a field.

I can speak legitimately about the mishandling of words which are my proper task. *In the beginning was the Word*, St John proclaims. Our latest version waters this down: *When all things began, the Word already was*, it says (as if things had begun on their own account). The change in itself is a tribute to mediocrity.

This and its like creep into our English garden, where yet Shakespeare is still not only read but enjoyed. A simple act of carpentry does it: the setting-up of the Bed of Procrustes.

The sea lies like violets below the road from Megara to Corinth, and there the young lad Theseus killed Procrustes, the robber baron, with his father's sword, and threw him down into that sea. The infamous bed, into which unlucky travellers had been fitted, either by stretching if they were short or by amputation if they were tall, was destroyed; but the fame of it has journeyed down the ages, and in one form or another it is still in use today.

It was obviously serviceable to Uniformity, and adopted when literature as well as other things became organized on the basis of supply and demand, which must of course always have been a foundation of production: the modern innovation was not a novelty in itself, but an inversion: the supply, which used to be offered by the author out of his head and accepted by his public if he were successful, is now conceived in answer to the public's own demand, its spontaneity restricted to what is held to be the man in the street's desire. The bed of Procrustes provides an immense paper army all marching in step and all bound – from our advertisements to our Bible – by their common objective – a language that without effort or imagination the dullest can understand. I have just been given a gramophone simplification of Dante's *Divine Comedy*, read in small fragments with far too long stretches of commentary between; the hope no doubt is that this may lead to the enjoyment of Dante himself, the second-rate to the first, but it does not do so: meanwhile the greatest literature can scarcely be trusted to speak for itself.

This is the more poignant when one remembers that words are the only arteries of thought our poor human body possesses; when the bed of Procrustes has finished with them, nothing but a thin trickle can drip through to give the average man (if there is such a one-eyed Cyclops) what he has asked for; made incapable of rising above the average man's level, the result is mediocrity not in words only but in thought as well.

That Shakespeare escapes is the wonder of our time. The English current, the strongest of its kind since the voice of ancient Greece was interrupted, runs deep, and still shows itself in much except the imaginatively creative side of literature. But it is just here that the average should be kept for what it is – a floor, tolerably smooth, but on no account built up to be a ceiling.

As for the young, they must somehow or other find steadfastness as we all have had to do, the quality essential for survival. We held, in our lost past, that only training or suffering could find it; but thought can also do most things, and can do them now. Youth must think hard, and may walk free, its feet on a mediocre and perhaps improving floor, but its head as high as may be in the clouds. If it meets Procrustes, and the Average tries to confound it, let it draw its weapon and remember that Theseus too was young.

1967

The zodiac arch was closing rather sadly when my publisher asked for an essay on the building of my house, and persuaded me to end with this last, or all but last, adventure – a private coracle still afloat on a current that has had too many war years in its darker patches. Molecules of history, millions of private lives, pass brightly through ages that live in our text books thick with gloom; and it is a comfort to remember that there have always been quiet places while nations and whole civilizations slid away.

> Felix qui potuit rerum cognoscere causas,
> Atque metus omnis et inexorabile fatum
> Subiecit pedibus strepitumque Acherontis avari:

These and those following were my favourite lines when I read Vergil; they have helped me through life and they keep their place; for we stand on our own feet in spite of all, and nothing need make us bow if we trust our own foundations.

Montoria

My parents were contemplating houses, somewhere, ever since I can remember. England particularly appears with a background of rather stolid men under bowler hats pushed too far up their foreheads, pulling out papers and discussing plans: and long rides followed, propped in front of my father on his bicycle to visit whatever he was building. Even when this had been done and we were peacefully installed, for some years perhaps, the feeling was one of mobility: a new staircase or a bathroom or a stable was being added; and, when there was nothing to be done in the house, my father would come in to breakfast on a summer's morning, and prudently looking at the children for sympathy where he knew he could find it, would remark that he was thinking of digging out a new pond down there by the copse.

All this should have produced a firm terrestrial feeling, but it has not: three houses of my own, since, have filled my life with every sort of delight except that of permanence; and I sometimes think that the continual early shifting of the domestic landscape rather than any unescapable urge of my own turned me into a nomad as my father was in his heart, no doubt, before me. The substance of this feeling is by no means restlessness, or escapism, or anything belonging to the fashionable psychology: it is simply that in a mobile world it seems natural as breathing to build a shelter to enjoy what views of it one likes – as a silkworm perhaps selects a twig for his cocoon while the butterfly stage is on its way.

Oh happy world where this could be done (and it was not a question of finance for we never had much to do it with): one saw a patch of field that looked out on Elysium and bought and planned it, and never a permit was asked for: and as I now remember very well, it was always the landscape and not the house itself that came first in our thoughts. You have there a difference between true architects who plan elaborate homes, and your nomad who merely likes his comfort as far as he can get it while enjoying the background.

In these last years I have built a house myself and feel as permanent in it as I can feel anywhere; yet I know that if I had to leave it – provided it were not for such squalor as might make the contrast unbearable – I would not unduly regret. Its memory would remain intact like a fly in amber, while the wonder of the world, greater than any personal possession, continues to wash around, with a tide far stronger than any anchor of my own natural or manufactured: the climate of unity is greater than any streak of peculiarity or exclusion, so that the idea of separation both with people and objects loses reality, as if all were enclosed in the same dewdrop and liable at any time to coalesce. This receptive atmosphere, so desirable yet apparently not natural to the United Nations for instance, gives the pleasure of ownership without that of possession and makes the use of things, and not their title-deeds, the main attraction. One is in fact a guest for life, in spite of all obstacles, on the beautiful surface of earth.

For three years nevertheless my house and I have been all in all to each other, since we met on a spring morning in 1963.

Strictly speaking, the house was not there: only a small grassy hill of terraces, now obliterated, for vines or olives which the unusually cold winter of 1929 destroyed. In May it was all grass, with a clump here and there of rosemary and a jonquil or two to speak of former owners, and a pan of their lost cottage on the slope. The top of the hill had evidently been a gun-emplacement in the first world war, and a narrow dug-out ran from it underground, warm and dry for some long black harmless snakes that shared the hill with lizards as green and swift as the emerald flash of the sun when it sinks in the tropics; minor lizards inhabited the few stony outcrops, and black and yellow spotted salamanders crept out from damp corners when it rained. All these I came to know later, and the birds also who, for the first year or two, never realized that this house had come to sit among them, and would fly in and out through the open windows; a bat came flitting through the door where I was standing, and settled upside down in the handle of an old Greek vase.

At first however there was nothing to see here but the hill and all its grasses filled with flowers. A little higher than the small monticules scattered about us, it dipped on every side to miniature woods and cuplike valleys, where the steps of the year could be followed through maize fields and hay slopes and rows of vines. Beyond, the whole beauty of North Italy spread as the painters have seen it — Monte Grappa in the north sucking up the landscape like a wave gathered to break, and on our south the Venetian plain with its hazy horizons clustered with villages and spires as if they were bees. On the east the castle and little town of Asolo rose from a dip where foothills of the Dolomites ran towards Belluno, and showed in farther gap the higher mountain snows; and on the west, close up against us as a foreground, on the only hill taller than ours, a small church of pilgrimage painted bright red, with steeple and church-house separate beside it, among cypresses and poplars on the site of the vanished castle of Frederic II's Ghibelline friends, the Ezzelini, who came there grimly to their end.

Beyond all this, beyond the half-seen towers of Bassano, were presences that came and went according to the weather, long snowy ridges of Vicenza mountains, or, on the opposite horizon, Venice in the glitter of her lagoon. In the far south, equally elusive unless the air were sharpened by frost or rain, were the Euganaean hills.

I had come up here without any intention of building or moving from my home in Asolo, to help some friends with thoughts of a holiday base. We had asked the *geometra* who dealt in lands to show us what he had: he had two little hills and this was one of them, and my guests preferred the other; they felt uncomfortable, they said, with half the world spread like Tintoretto's Last Judgement before them, and they bought their more intimate height straightaway, quite near by and in sight.

But I spent a week making up my mind — or rather going through the ritual natural to those in love, whose reason has to be adjusted to something which has already happened. There was as yet no thought of a house, since I had my own; but I felt anxious to rescue the stupendous view from some unworthy fate, a pseudo-Palladian vandal for instance: and as it happened I had five thousand pounds loose in my possession at the moment. Money, I feel in spite of all experience, is only safe when it is spent. The sum had come to me from the sale of some pictures, and was on its way to be saved from me and my expenditure by investment in an annuity – but it had not yet started, and I began to think of the hill too in a light of Investment. This last green unspoilt fringe of the Lombard-Venetian plain is bound to grow more valuable as industry thickens in the hot flat stretches below, and how delightful as well as profitable it would be to see one's property gain month by month or year by year in value, to catch up with the annuity in the end.

After a week, the *geometra* and I called on the owner – a charming, peppery gentleman-farmer whose sons were uninterested and lands gently decreasing – and in the middle of an argument between demo-Christian and liberal policies, over a bottle of the excellent wine of his vines which he said I might soon be emulating – our agreement was drawn up and signed. The final form, in language arranged for tax collectors when the money is actually paid over, came a very few days later, and left me free of all my sight could master, as I lay under one of the mulberry trees whose leaves had fed forgotten silkworms on the hill of Montoria, now my own.

The next step followed, unsure but inevitable, swiftly advancing through the helpless breastworks of reason. Was it to be a shed for summer picnics while the Investment made its way? or a room to write in? or a shelter for week-ends? or a home altogether, to be built through the sale of the old one which now, in Asolo, was in the centre of a boom? The steps of the ladder of desire are quickly climbed. I could build the new, I calculated, with half of what the old would sell for, and keep the surplus for that annuity on which the comfort of my old age depended. I bought some squared paper and drew a plan. The *geometra* produced an estimate which eventually covered a little less than the third of the cost and mopped up every penny I possessed apart from my old house.

A young lad with a bulldozer came to toss out a platform on my hill. His machine, browsing like a dinosaur with mouthfuls of grass that left red lips of soil where they touched, cut the road out in a day, straight up the slope 'like an arowe clere.' It is now a double stretch of porphyry stone with grass between, dry in all weathers, with an absence of curve that gives one's car a small though uneventful imitation of a tightrope. Before these finishing touches were given, lorries began to come up loaded with sand, gravel, bricks, cement and girders – and this they continued to do for the next two years.

I got no architect, but sat at my (imaginary) desk in my (imaginary) house and drew its contours round me, and have come to the conclusion that this is the right way to build for living – from inside outwards and not from outside in; 'I thinks,' said the child, 'and then I draws round what I thinks'. The *geometra* had these thoughts drawn out in a suitable form for government approval, continuing to mislead me at a third of their cost; and the builder, standing slightly askew so as to distribute his plumpness to the best advantage, would then correct any structural impossibility. He is an excellent builder and the local peasants are good masons and make their own houses, and they were pleased because I wanted thick walls of faded bricks mixed with stone, in the old-fashioned way of this countryside. The stone they quarry from the hillside here is almost marble, and window-sills and eaves and flooring of portico or stairs are all chipped out of it, rose-coloured or white or pale yellow as we chose it. Over the entrance, which is open and floored with the pink stone, the cutter carved a line from Dante's *Purgatorio: Noi siam peregrin come voi siete* (we are pilgrims as you are), for a greeting to those who may come.

All this went on happily, and I had no misgivings. The old home, I thought, would sell with no trouble, and went off to Turkey that same summer to read Roman history, hoping it might do so in my absence. When I came back, a slump which the Italians officially and ridiculously called a *congiuntura* – a disjuncture if ever there was one – had settled on the country, paralysing everything for the next two years and practically annihilating my chances of a sale.

The *geometra*, full of a mothlike charm that never quite burnt his wings, was interested in politics only, and hardly to be found beside the work he was by way of superintending. The water supply he had promised stopped far short of the house and its pipe was half the size it should be. The electric light, which had some way to walk along a charming valley, needed a great deal of local government influence to make it do so; and the workmen had to be paid every week. In these months my friends with scarcely an exception agreed that I was mad. They begged me to stop while there was time, cut my losses, and settle in my old home, and they argued with an anxiety that showed so much affection that I think of it with tenderness today. But my dreams were on the other side, and which is more real, we or they? My hill was spoilt now, full of hideous gashes and bruises that would sink with their rudiments into squalor if I left it; the thought of a bit of the earth's surface wantonly wrecked, combined with the reflection that I would be left penniless, made me decide to carry on as planned.

I did what I could, promising three times the usual commission to anyone who managed to sell my old home. In the *geometra*'s absence I went every day and watched, hypnotised, while something like a Frankenstein rose from the drawings on squared paper that had looked so unassuming. As the place was at that time considered so lonely as to be almost uninhabitable (wild people, the Asolo citizens all said!) I had planned a double house with a flat to let, for company, on my ground floor; and this, which has turned out to be sound, added to our size and dignity. But all the money I had was by now literally down the drains of these foundations. I smothered my doubts and studied the shapes of arches, plain and yet noble enough to surround the dream: the builder and I would experiment, while two workmen held a plank higher or lower to see where the spring of the arch should begin.

Every day, from morning to night, the amateur builder must come to his decisions – things he knows nothing about, like life itself – a matter of construction, ignorant, but hopefully secure: there is no waiting to find out, when the men have to be paid. I became expert in things I had never met before, and devoted to the workmen who, if they happened to be interested, found their way round every problem as it came. In my first optimism over the estimates I had designed a marble balcony and marble bathrooms; it was too late to retrench, and this extravagance – like so many others – continues to give me pleasure today.

During the second year, when already the roof was on and things like floors and windows were being fitted, the clouds of the *congiuntura* increased. People waited in Asolo, hoping to buy my old home, like vultures in the gauntness of Asia. Small businesses were 'liquidating' all around; and the bank, from which I had been forced to borrow all they would give me, sent silky little notes, on rose-coloured paper, every four months to remind me of an interest that, with one thing and another, climbed steeply near to ten per cent a year.

Friends were very good in this time of my distress, and a gift and two loans came winging unasked across the sea, saving me from the pathological suavity of the banks. Such acts are not to be forgotten and do much to tilt the balance of life happily in favour of the poor, and though everyone who cared for me was by this time showing signs of distress, I remained comparatively cheerful so long as I kept away from reckonings. The airy absences of my *geometra*, making it necessary for me to stay on the job and come to all its decisions myself, helped very greatly; so did the fact that I was planting olive rows and fruit trees, soothing millennial things. I reflected that most of the world lives thus, on its own feet from day to day with the abyss beside it, and is not unduly frightened. If the worst came to the worst, I would still have enough to pay the workmen, and the world with all its possibilities and freedoms would be my home. The nomad quality of my house-building came to my assistance, and I remember that in those two years of trial I only three times took a tranquillizer at night, when sleep was being killed by the fierceness of arithmetic.

My green hill, so rich in flowers – hellebores, anemones, orchids, and lilies grow wild there, and cyclamen and Christmas roses were naturalized already, with lilies of the valley in the shade – was now disfigured on all sides with dumps of yellow earth. It was peopled by ant-like rows of diggers in the sun, gloomily reminiscent of the pyramids. They filled endless buckets with waste earth, which a crane deposited on the hilltop, raising the contour of the district by seven feet and giving me, as it happened, a fifth most splendid view. Three large cisterns were dug into the soil there and two more had to be rolled to their various places: not a drop of our mountain water could we squander.

The summer of 1964 went pleasantly in spite of the financial dead-lock. New trees were growing all over my ten acres and a few energetic friends descended now and then from their alpine holidays to dig about among them. The swimming pool, which had filled my publisher with despair, was bulldozed, dynamited, and finally completed before the warm days ceased; it had a border of the good white stone, and a little demi-lune of red water-lilies at each end. 'You can't have water-lilies and a swimming pool together', my friends kept on saying: but of course one can, by putting a wall up to water level between! The pool is high, and looks over the country as one swims. As soon as it was done, we bathed and picnicked on its border, regardless of the chaos that still surrounded it; and the young workmen would take a dip before they left in the evening. Friends camped in the small folly beside it that has a bedroom and shower, where we could sit after sunset on a small terrace and watch swallows fly from far and near to the rareness of water, stitching their swift tapestry and drinking as they dipped. The birds sail down here in the draught of the Brenner valley, and used to be caught in the two copses on my hill and in others near by, that were called *roccoli* and planted as bird-trapping mazes with a decoy in a cage to lure them down. 'You cannot think how I love the birds,' my farming neighbour told me: 'I shoot them every Sunday.' His *roccolo* has now been bought by friends of mine and the birds are free in our oasis, and hoopoes and orioles have shown themselves, and nightingales sing in the copse. Because I am above the treetops, I see them drop downwards, smoothly with open wings, outside my bedroom windows.

The winter of 1964 came with desperate frustration, for my new house stood ready, its stone-cut staircase easy, its few rooms pleasant but empty, and I dared not furnish it, or dismantle the Asolo home before a sale. The slump was getting worse instead of better, and extending to England. The English agents wrote with expensive cheerfulness about their advertisement, which had produced fifty answers but no visitors except one in search of a tiny cottage, so that I became embittered about agents. I was now asking only half of what I had expected in the boom, and saw a vast deficit ahead of me even if I could sell. The sums I had to deal with were so large that even now they scarcely find their way into my understanding: they gave me sleepless nights, when I looked at myself with surprise, as if I were a stranger.

A small coincidence not only enabled me to furnish my house, but nearly smoothed out the deficit as well.

A retired dentist and his wife set up an antique shop just opposite my gates in Asolo, and as they prospered and became cluttered up with their stock of beds and chairs and wardrobes, I offered them the use of my rooms as showrooms; every piece of furniture they brought in enabled me to take one of my own away, and a gradual translation went on all through the winter. As I, too, would have to get rid of a good deal of furniture for want of room, I offered them a commission on anything they sold together with their own. This worked very well, though it made the unexpectedness of life even more apparent, since the table one was eating at was liable at a day's notice to be swept away. By some weird economic law, the prices of antique furniture rise when everything is sinking, and by the end of the winter I had poured half my deficit into the laps of carpenters and plumbers – helpful to our common morale. I had always thought of shopkeeping as dull, but it now showed itself to be full of variety and drama, bringing the unknown to one's threshold with every customer. Some were engaging and talked with human interest about themselves and the objects they were carrying away; others would seek out every flaw in the poor old pieces that had kept me happy and contented from my youth, until I felt thankful that no one speaks in such a way about one's face. It was surprising to what wormlike manoeuvres expensively dressed people would descend, and I found myself thinking nostalgically of the formal and dignified bargaining of the East. But on the whole I enjoyed the plunge into so new an experience, and developed, I think, a toughness hitherto kept for major crises in exploration. By the middle of May the mountain was completely furnished and what was left in Asolo had nearly all been sold. But the old house, no longer lived in and now rather sad in its borrowed trappings, was as marooned as ever.

The summer passed, the *congiuntura* continued, eating its way into all private lives, and it was autumn before a ray of financial hope appeared unexpectedly from the provincial council of Treviso, which had a government grant to invest in cultural sites. My house, its garden the only piece of flat ground in Asolo, was in the running. Under a smooth and apparently simple exterior a submerged and complicated game of chess was being played between the delegates of the council and all the small towns that had houses to dispose of, and though my house was as good as any and indeed better chosen for its site than most, the triple commission offered for its sale no doubt helped, though not as absolutely as the cynics hold. 'Money,' my friend the *geometra* remarked when we discussed these philosophies, 'is not sufficient for happiness, but it is indubitably good for the nerves.'

The battle in the provincial council went on into October and was finally decided in my favour. A last discord was settled by the Prefect, a fair-minded, office-worn man whom we visited in person – for in all this long Odyssey I was helped by my friends both high and low. The delegates when they came to sign talked about Greek vases and old faience in the happy Italian way that slips into civilization when it can; the contract was ratified and the difficult point of immediate payment was gained to the surprise of the whole province, where the council has never been known to pay with such unofficial speed. Feeling on top of the world at last, or at least on the top of my hill, I went off for a holiday in Rome and found a telegram to say that the sale was cancelled: my old house had been requisitioned by the Allied Military Government at the end of the war and never derequisitioned; most of the Asolo houses, it went on to say, were in the same condition.

This was almost too much, but it was a short agony. A general edict of release was discovered, thoughtfully issued by the Allied Military before they left. An earlier requisition perpetrated by the Italian Fascists on enemy property in 1940 was again discovered by the provincial council, and also frustrated. 'If the Nazis had requisitioned the Vatican, would that still hold?' I asked, but the question was frivolous and the crisis over. My cheque was paid early in the year and allowed me to break very nearly even when all my debts were paid; and the sum I had when all this Odyssey began was promptly sent to Switzerland by a kind bank manager at a time when the black market in Italy could operate on semi-legal lines of its own.

A last incident has yet to be told.

In the height of my troubles I promised my guardian angel (unknown to me but I hope existent), to build him a shrine at the bottom of my hill when the last debt was paid. The moment came, and a year ago the shrine was built. 'It seems to me,' I said to Emma, my cook, who has spent her life with us, 'that we are treating the angel well, and he, or she, or it, might find out for us the thief who stole my jewels', for during the ten months or so when we lived partly in one house and partly in the other my jewel box had disappeared. Emma has always had it in her keeping, but she was confused and could remember nothing and had not seen it for months. Both houses were ransacked, and theft seemed the only explanation. I could not tell the police as that would have meant serious trouble for Emma, so nothing was said till the angel and his obligations brought the matter up again. No response was noticed from the shrine, which is small and pretty, a whitewashed little apse by the roadside with a magnolia and a cypress planted on either side. In the spring of this year Maxwell Armfield came to stay and painted the angel on a sword in a blue sky, with a staff in one hand and my house in the crook of his other arm. When his face and wind-blown yellow hair were painted, the jewel box was discovered in the old house, hidden behind the kitchen sink of all unsuitable places, either by a miracle or by Emma, according to the temper of one's mind.

Soon after this our Monsignor of the red church blessed the shrine and the peasants came around to wish luck to us and it with wine under the trees.

The hill is now settled in its life of everyday with a foreign breath now and then blowing through the haymaking or wood-cutting of its seasons. I love it dearly, the more so because it keeps its natural laws — the garden shrubs and flowers grow as if by chance in grassy places. It is still a nomad house although so solidly built, like those of my parents before me; one is not cramped by its walls even when one lives inside them, but feels rather that country business and rippling horizons wash in and out through windows wide and low. The proportions of life are kept, not severed from a world that they survey: so that I can think of my home as a tent to be enjoyed, and left, whenever the moment comes.

1967

Notes

Royal Tombs at Mycenae

1. Deciphered in 1952. See *The Decipherment of Linear B* by John Chadwick (CUP)

The Golden Domes of Iraq and Iran

1. Sir William Muir, *The Caliphate: Rise, Decline and Fall*, pp. 307ff.
2. Ibid.
3. Ibid.
4. The murdered king and regent of Iraq were descended from the Prophet.
5. The month of Ramadhan, the ninth month of the year and the Muslim equivalent of Lent, is given over to fasting by day; but the night is full of celebrations, and the mosques and minarets are illuminated.

Lunch with Homer

1. *The Present State of the Islands in the Archipelago* (Oxford, 1687).
2. *Odyssey* Book III: Chapman's translation.

Time

1. Sir Walter Raleigh.

On Silence

1. A gulley, usually ice.

Our Second-rate Security

1. *Paradise Lost*, Book 1, 278–83.

List of Sources

THE FOREIGN OFFICE DROPS ITS 'H'—*The Baghdad Times*, 8.12.1932

PERSIAN LEGENDS—*The Cornhill Magazine*, Spring 1931

IDEAS AND THE MANDATE—*Time and Tide*, 31.10.1936

HIMYAR, THE LIZARD: 1938—*Chamber's Journal*, December 1944

A NOTE ON STYLE—Lecture to the Secondary School in Baghdad, 1942

EXPLORING WITH WORDS—*The Listener*, 30.1.1947

TRAVEL FOR SOLITUDE—*The Spectator*, 24.3.1950

SAYING WHAT ONE MEANS—*The Cornhill Magazine*, Summer 1963

MY WORST JOURNEY: 1943—*The Geographical Magazine*, April 1954

THE WISE MEN—*Time and Tide*, 5.12.1953

ROUND PERIM IN WARTIME—*The Quarterly Review*, October 1940

ARAB BACKGROUND—*The Quarterly Review*, January 1949

THE BULL-FIGHT—*The Spectator*, 18.11.1949

TIDINESS—*Time and Tide*, 10.12.1949

GREED—*Time and Tide*, 5.5.1951

THIS I BELIEVE—BBC programme for the USA, 1953

THE TRAVELLING READER—*The Geographical Magazine*, December 1958

TRAVELLING WITH A NOTEBOOK—*The Cornhill Magazine*, Spring 1954

THE TRAVEL ESSAY—*The Cornhill Magazine*, Summer 1965

TUNISIA FOR THE TOURIST, *Vogue*, August 1961

THE GOLDEN DOMES OF IRAQ AND IRAN—*The Cornhill Magazine*, Spring 1961

LUNCH WITH HOMER—*Encounter*, March 1968

PASSING FASHIONS—*Homes and Gardens*, May 1968

IN DEFENCE OF SMUGGLING—*Holiday*, October 1966

TIME—by courtesy of Mr. Ned O'Gorman

ON SILENCE—*The Cornhill Magazine*, Autumn 1966

OUR SECOND-RATE SECURITY—*The Times*, 25.3.1967

DECADENCE, OR THE BED OF PROCRUSTES—*The Times*, 28.8.1967

MONTORIA—*The Cornhill Magazine*, Winter 1967–8